7.50

EBURY PRESS
BHAGWAAN KE PAKWAAN

Devang Singh was blessed with an agile understanding of light which inspired him to leave his history degree aside to become a photographer, director and producer—a profession that has yielded both content for brands worldwide and near life-ending encounters with lone tuskers.

Varud Gupta was born and bred for business until a brusque millennial existential crisis sent him travelling through the culinary cultures of the world. He's been a NY cheesemonger, an Argentine asador, a Peruvian bartender and a spy in countless household kitchens.

PRAISE FOR BHAGWAAN KE PAKWAAN

'*Bhagwaan ke Pakwaan* takes us on an exciting journey that explores faith, cuisine and culture from across the country. With the help of beautifully captured pictures and the bonus of traditional recipes for one to try at home, this book is a homage to India's rich culinary heritage and diversity'—Shashi Tharoor

'If there's a God and He lays his hands on a copy of *Bhagwaan ke Pakwaan*, he would I am sure roar with laughter, working up a healthy appetite. Devang Singh and Varud Gupta play a culinary duet to perfection, with a refreshingly light touch and a sparkling sense of humour. Others have written about the Chhappan Bhog and Sacred Foods offered to gods in myriad temples across the length and breadth of this land, but most seem to groan under the burden of gravitas. None have dared to include in their researched tomes favourite foods of tribal deities—Flesh, Fish and Fowl. What a delight it is to encounter blessed delicacies that are prepared in Parsi agiaries and Jewish synagogues! The authors have led fascinating lives and are gifted with enchanting visual imagination. With a few well-chosen words, they transport us to exotic tribal homelands as well as the hallowed precincts of the legendary Jagannath temple. Absolutely unputdownable. To be dipped in ritualistically at regular intervals'—Pushpesh Pant

'Both ambitious and unique in scope, *Bhagwaan Ke Pakwaan* serves up a witty take on the intersection of food and faith in India, and along the way the hidden cuisines to be discovered on this spectacular journey'—Gul Panag

'This wonderfully quirky book is a heady cocktail of culture, history and cuisine that showcases that there's a lot more to food than what we eat'—Abish Mathew

'An absolute masterpiece that takes you into the depths of tribal ceremonies and intimate rituals. The pictures are outstanding. And as someone who is deeply connected with the north-east, the first chapter transported me home. Eager to see what's next on this journey!'— Chef Saby

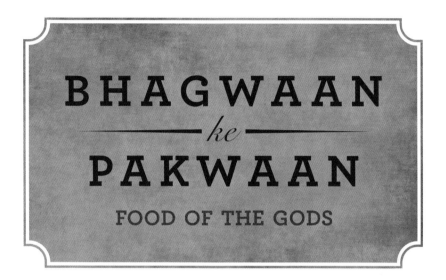

BHAGWAAN
ke
PAKWAAN

FOOD OF THE GODS

VARUD GUPTA | DEVANG SINGH

EBURY
PRESS

An imprint of Penguin Random House

EBURY PRESS

USA | Canada | UK | Ireland | Australia
New Zealand | India | South Africa | China

Ebury Press is part of the Penguin Random House group of companies
whose addresses can be found at global.penguinrandomhouse.com

Published by Penguin Random House India Pvt. Ltd
7th Floor, Infinity Tower C, DLF Cyber City,
Gurgaon 122 002, Haryana, India

First published in Ebury Press by Penguin Random House India 2019

Copyright © Devang Singh and Varud Gupta 2019
Written by Varud Gupta
Photography by Devang Singh
Additional photography by Yash Pal Singh

10 9 8 7 6 5 4 3 2 1

While every effort has been made to verify the authenticity of the information
contained in this book, the publisher and the author are in no way liable for
the use of the information contained herein.

ISBN 9780143444626

Typeset in Archer and Avenir Next
Book design by Parag Chitale
Printed at Replika Press Pvt. Ltd, India

www.penguin.co.in

To bellies around the world—of all shapes, sizes and faiths

WHAT'S COOKING

PROLOGUE

Hello there.

Welcome. It's great to meet you, book-to-face.
You might be standing at the store, lying in a hammock, or
reading this book years from now when Earth has come to a
cataclysmic yet predictable end and you're piecing together
the remaining fragments of humanity with a small band of
survivors, and thinking, 'What? *Bhagwaan ke Pakwaan*? What's
this all about?'

Well, that's what prologues are for.

Firstly, 'Bhagwaan ke Pakwaan' loosely translates to 'Food
of the Gods'. Hopefully that's a good first step towards
understanding what you have in your hands. We titled it so
because it's just catchier in Hindi.

Secondly, if you're expecting a traditional cookbook then
you can stop right here (or, if experiencing the third scenario,
get your priorities in order). Because this book, like most
of human existence, is a hotchpotch journey that can't be
defined by a single genre.

Oh sorry! We skipped a step.

Let us introduce ourselves first. I—as in one half of the 'us',
whose names are on the front cover—am Varud Gupta, the
writer. The other I is Devang Singh, who clicked buttons
resulting in the majestic pictures that follow.

Bhagwaan ke Pakwaan began with a small idea between two
foodies: how can we explore the culture and cuisine of this
country without ripping off someone else's idea? And in India,
there are no two more important facets of life than religion
and food.

But—religion in India? That's tricky.

Especially when you consider that between the two of us, one's a confused atheist and the other a procrastinating agnostic. So why in *God's name* are these two people making this book? Because we swear to the God we don't believe in or the God we can't know (respectively), we were simply fascinated by the stories we came upon and decided to tell here.

Did you catch all that? Wait, don't reply out loud. We can't hear you and people will think you're crazy. But take a moment to digest this. We have all the time in the world.

Traditionally, when talking about this area of food-meets-faith, people might think of what's known as *bhog*, or food specifically offered to Gods—but that's a narrow outlook and quite frankly unfair to both cuisine and religion. There's more to the picture: how faith can inform the food of a community and, surprisingly enough, how food can in turn influence faith.

The Zoroastrians have food that is prepared for the souls of the departed. In Spiti, due to a history of scarcity, some Buddhist monks still consume meat. When the Baghdadi Jews came to India, local ingredients added quirks to their kosher diet. The Temples of Odisha beat to the rhythm of *chhappan bhog*: fifty-six dishes prepared daily for the Lord of the Universe, Jagannath. And in the Karbi tribe, rice, especially rice beer, is the lifeblood of the community.

You are now running out of time. You've been awkwardly holding this book for too long. You're thinking, 'Should I buy you? Are you worth my time?'

We know your time is precious, but we also know you're different from everyone else. You're edgy. Original. You want something before the masses have leeched it. Everyone has already watched *Sacred Games*; what do you want to do? Be a follower, or a trendsetter?

Maybe you'll learn something from this book. Perhaps try a
recipe or two. Maybe you'll appreciate a culture more the
next time you travel. Maybe on Tinder, your match will have a
quote from this book in their bio and then—BAM!—love at first
swipe. Or perhaps, if, like us, you are equally confused when it
comes to faith, this could be that step forward.

Worst case, buy this book and carry it around with you. Throw
on a pair of glasses. You'll immediately seem like a more
interesting person. And that's all worth it in itself, right?

RONGMESEK, MEGHALAYA
KARBI TRIBE

A scene from the movie *Ratatouille*: A tall, lanky man walks into a classy French establishment and opens the menu. His name is Anton Ego. The waiter, Mustafa, walks in.

Mustafa: Do you know what you'd like this evening, sir?

Anton Ego: Yes, I think I do. After reading a lot of overheated puffery about your new cook, you know what I'm craving? A little perspective. That's it. I'd like some fresh, clear, well-seasoned perspective. Can you suggest a good wine to go with that?

Mustafa: With what, sir?

Anton Ego: Perspective. Fresh out, I take it?

Mustafa: I am, uh . . .

Perspective was what was on our minds as we rumbled along the dirt paths into Rongmesek, our last stop of this journey. It's hard to come by these days.

With all the advances in technology one would think that we've become more global of a community, when the reality is that we're still living in bubbles—from newsfeeds to friend circles—huddled together in Plato's cosy cave.

But as we turned away from the concrete and into a lush wilderness tucked behind the hills of Meghalaya, a Karbi tribal community changed all that. Before we knew it, it had started. That indescribable ooey-gooey warm brownie feeling deep in our souls in a week that began with an animal sacrifice and ended with a fashion show.

There's a lot going on in this community straddled between a traditional past and modern future. Perspective is ripe and served daily.

SPIRITS
OF LIFE

As with most days in Ri-Bhoi, there was a glass of rice beer in our hands before we trekked behind Albinus Timug, the head of this *riad*, or village-state, to one of the sixteen communities on the outskirts. (It's quite possible that we accidentally called him Albus a couple times. Although unfortunately not a wizard, he was equally eccentric.)

It was there that we would witness a ceremony only imaginable in a Hogwarts Divination class: a reading of entrails. But before we could take our seats Albinus spotted our bamboo mugs were empty and called for a refill, an offer we couldn't refuse.

A chicken slowly bled to death in the hands of one of the village elders who chanted from the depths of his throat.

Next to us sat Dr Fabian Lyngdoh—also with a bamboo mug of rice beer—translating the local Khasi dialect of the man to his right (he wasn't having any rice beer so we question his judgment).

The ritual that was unfolding in front of us was one that falls under 'animism' or an indigenous faith sometimes referred to as Ancient Hinduism—but due to the variety of influences from East Asia, these titles are mere political classifications rather than a true reflection of the faith. What exists here is a rich and robust tradition with unique mythologies such as the mythical bird, *voplakpi*, that propagated mankind.

Before the elder were two gourds—representing two deities, or Spirits of Nature. According to myth, one of these deities, Peng, was at first a wild, evil 'forest entity' with a proclivity for trickery. After mankind tamed him, he took his spot above their doorways, protecting them from other malevolent spirits as the new household guardian (in exchange for the occasional meal).[1]

The ceremony continued as the elder placed the chicken at the foot of these deities and brought out a bamboo mug of his own. These deities were being called upon through these prayers to aid in the village's request, to ensure a successful start to the sowing cycle that would begin the next day. He sprinkled the rice beer on to the gourds, inviting the deities to give their blessing. After this, he made an incision in the chicken's rear end to pull out the entrails. Took a moment with them. Then finally announced that the ceremony had been a success—how he determined so was not something we were made privy to.

But the village elder wasn't alone in that decision. To help him, he had, at the very beginning, also called upon his ancestors, another important facet of their faith. From deities to ancestral spirits, these communities pay homage to their lineage as well as nature, fostering a connectedness to the world around them.

The offering of rice beer represents their gratitude, but no ceremony can end without feeding the deities. The chicken, along with rice used in the ceremony, was then cooked and served to the deities before parting ways.

VILLAGE ON FIRE

Some traditions, however, fade with time. The vibes of the main town of Rongmesek are more modern. And smack dab in the middle is a church.

Our story begins in Rome, 1889. A religious congregation—the Society of the Divine Saviour—is preparing to send the German Father Otto Hopfenmuller to Assam to indoctrinate communities into their faith. Otto makes his way over to Shillong where his first few months are spent learning the tribal culture and translating Christian scriptures into Khasi[2].

The legend goes, as Dr Fabian's brother, Constantine, narrates, that there once was a village called Phahamingding, or the village on fire. For years a great mystery had plagued the residents: every spring, a fire would ravage the village, destroying land and houses alike. Until one fortunate day a French priest encountered this village and baptized its community into the Catholic faith, and suggested they rename the village to Rongmesek. Then— the fires stopped.

But faith was only a pinch of what followed. A church was founded in the heart of the village, and a school at its side. Education led to improvements in language, agriculture, macro-economics and societal welfare. To appease the pessimist in you, crediting the new life of this village—away from magical fires—to education wouldn't be a stretch.

Today, Sunday mass has become an ingrained part of the lifestyle with the entire town closing for the day. While the Catholic doctrines might not have changed, the spirit of Karbi culture has affected how Christian practices manifest themselves in this once burning village: during mass, traditional dances are a part of the ceremony. The custom of blessing grains with the ceremonies of the indigenous faith continues in its own fashion at the church.

Constantine finds an enthusiasm behind the newfound Christian faith. There's a joy that this once isolated village has now become part of a bigger community. Whether wrong or right, everything that happened has led to this moment for the village. We have no control over the past. There is no point in regret.

Whether it was truly a miracle, coincidence or simply strategic planning—ultimately faith is what you make of it. And in this community, it served as a step forward. In the month of August, prayers are dedicated to India with the national flag proudly swaying inside the church.

Becoming Christian has made this community no less Indian.

OF RICE AND MEN

At this point, we'd officially had more rice beer than water. So we decided it would be wise to learn more about the liquid carbs, or *hor arak*, we'd been consuming copiously. Rice has been an integral part of Karbi culture and religion since time immemorial.

Side note: we picked up a life-hack in Meghalaya when we noticed a certain phrase being used often–*time immemorial*. The saying refers to a time beyond memory or record, which is relevant here since written tradition and a sense of Karbi identity didn't emerge in the community until India's pre-Independence days[3].

But it's also a nifty way to sound smart while trying to cover up the fact that you actually don't know when something happened.

So, it was *time immemorial* when the Karbi, of Tibeto-Burman ancestry from Western China or Central Asia headed to these hills seeking protection from Burmese invaders[4]. And until today, walk into any household kitchen and you'll find stalks of grain hung at the hearth as a token of the interaction between the village and their ancestors.

Rice was abundant in this new environment, and thus became the basis of their cuisine. In the forest, flora and fauna became nutrition–from pork, buffalo and chicken to insects and fish. Bountiful land served as paddy fields and bamboo groves became a pillar of the cuisine and lifestyle–bamboo is eaten, cooked in, fermented in, constructed with, burnt as fuel and, arguably most important, used to drink rice beer from.

'Rice beer is the one true food of the gods.'

Dr Fabian made that our motto while in Meghalaya. To the Karbi people, rice beer is the fuel that refreshes you with the sweet buzz of life. And, as he used to champion, 'It won't make you drunk . . . just lively.'

KARBI ESSENTIALS

Hello = **Hello**

Good morning (or First Greeting) = **Kardom**

How are you? = **Nangdum koson lo?**

Where's the bathroom? = **Kodak te do painkana?**

I love you = **Ne nang phan kang hom**

Goodbye = **Bye**

ZARA SA JHUM LOON

With its dependence on rice, it's no wonder that the Karbi lifestyle revolves around the harvest cycle. *Jhum* cultivation is the technique in which patches of land are cleared and burnt so that the mineral potash (one of the essentials for plant growth along with nitrogen and phosphorus) can be obtained from the ashes.

Then a mix of seeds from rice, maize and other vegetables is sown in that land to yield a variety of produce, hedging itself against any crop failure. This process begins in the spring with a festival that unites people of all faiths. It's quite the bash for the community, with singing, dancing and, obviously, rice beer.

But in recent years, there's been a strong push against Jhum cultivation due to concerns over pollution and the subsequent loss of a broader ecosystem in and around the burnt land. Meanwhile, modern techniques can now replace the mineral needs while resulting in bigger yields.

Like the rise of Christianity in Ri-Bhoi, the perceived loss of a traditional lifestyle can be disheartening to some. But if prosperity can be created by educating a community along a forward-looking path, who are we to judge.

EAT, PRAY, LOVE

One of the most impressive facets of the Karbi lifestyle is the very vivid sub-cultures that have developed over years within the community.

As the harvest cycle comes to an end, the village breaks out into day long celebrations, dances and general merrymaking. The dances are akin to Karbi speed dating where potential suitors get a chance to interact with the young women and a courtship might blossom.

As with dance, fashion is deeply embedded into the culture. With an economy built around textiles, we were treated to a fashion show where the village teens designed their own clothing lines, a wonderful blend of the integrity of their past traditions and the influence of modern trends.

CHICKEN WITH BAMBOO SHOOTS
(Serves 4)

Past Peng's watchful gaze, we enter the Karbi kitchen—the most sacred of domestic spaces—where the cuisine rests upon three cooking styles: Kang-moi or alkaline preparations which use ingredients such as banana bark or bamboo ash for the salt alkali; Ka-lang-dang or boiled preparations; and lastly, Han-thor, or sour preparations which dominate the cuisine. Here this can be seen in the use of fermented bamboo shoots[5].

The village traditionally uses fermented bamboo, but since it's hard to procure and production has decreased over time, we replaced it with the canned variety and adapted the recipe accordingly.

Ingredients
½ cup canned bamboo shoots
2 tbsp mustard oil

1 tbsp ginger, finely chopped
1 garlic clove, finely chopped
2–3 red onions, sliced thinly
2–3 green chillies, sliced
1 tsp turmeric
1 kg chicken (halved chunks of legs, thighs and wings)
½ cup rice powder
Salt to taste

Wash the bamboo shoots and boil in water for 10 minutes until tender. Drain the water and set the shoots aside.

Heat the mustard oil in a pan and fry up the bamboo shoots, about 3-4 minutes.

Add the ginger, garlic, onions and green chillies. Continue to sauté until they begin to brown.

Add the salt and turmeric.

Add the chicken pieces and let them brown for 4-5 minutes, before adding one cup water.

Continue to simmer until the chicken is cooked through, 7-8 minutes.

Slowly add the rice powder, a spoon at a time, until the gravy thickens. It should have a gelatinous consistency. Serve piping hot with rice.

PORK 'N' GREENS

(Serves 4)

From aiding in digestion to curing food poisoning and treating joint pains, medicinal plants play an important role in Karbi cuisine. But unless you have a botanist friend with access to such herbs as Lapong or *Ficus auriculata* (of the fig family), these might be hard to find and have been unfortunately substituted for more practical ingredients.

Ingredients

2 red onions, sliced thinly
2 garlic cloves
4–5 green chillies, sliced thinly
1 tbsp chopped ginger
3 tbsp mustard oil
1½ cup chopped spinach (or kale, mustard greens)
1 kg pork belly, roughly 2–3 cm chunks
Salt to taste
½ cup black sesame, roasted and ground

Mash the onions, garlic, chillies and ginger into a fine paste using a mortar and pestle (or grind in a blender).

Heat the mustard oil in a pan and sauté the paste until it browns for 2–3 minutes.

Add the chopped greens and stir until they wilt and release water. Keep stirring so they don't burn; add a little water if required.

(Optional: Banana ash would normally be added, rumored to soften the meat, making this dish a Kang-moi or alkali preparation. You can add ½ tbsp of vinegar instead.)

When your greens have wilted completely—they should be tender but not brown with still a bit of water in the pan—add the pork belly. This time will vary depending on which green you have used, roughly 10 minutes.

(Optional: You can mix in offal cuts of pork depending on your appetite for adventure. We, personally, love it.)

Add the pork while still sizzling along with the black sesame and salt.

Allow the pork to brown and the fat to render, roughly 3-4 minutes, before adding 1 ½ cups water.

Cook uncovered for 15-20 minutes, allowing the pork to fully cook and the gravy to thicken. Time might vary depending on which green you used. Serve piping hot to accompany the chicken and bamboo shoots with rice.

FISH COOKED IN BAMBOO
(Serves 4)

The original dish is a wonder that highlights the versatility of bamboo in Karbi cuisine—the fish is both prepared and cooked inside a bamboo shoot. This is the at-home method.

Ingredients

1 red onion, sliced
½ garlic clove
2–3 red chillies, sliced thinly
1 kg fatty fish with skin (salmon, snapper, Bombay duck), chopped into 2–3 cm chunks
1 tbsp salt
1 tsp turmeric
3 tbsp mustard oil
1 cup water
¼ cup coriander, whole leaves

Mash the onions, garlic and chillies together into a chunky paste (or grind in a blender).
Sear the pieces of fish in 2 tbsp mustard oil on high heat for 1–2 minutes, just long enough to render the fat and crisp up skin, without cooking the flesh.
Remove as many bones as possible from the fish using your hands—try not to break the pieces apart too much.
Heat the remaining oil in a pan and lightly sauté the onion, garlic and chilli paste over medium heat.

As the paste starts to brown, add the fish and water. Cover and cook for around 5–7 minutes; the fish should be cooked through but not dry.
Add the coriander leaves and let the curry simmer for 2–3 minutes more, covered. The gravy will be quite liquidy.
Serve hot with rice.

CICADA CHUTNEY

(Serves 4)

If you don't know this already, twenty years down the road we might be looking at insects for a large portion of the protein in our diet. Nicknamed the 'World Cup Insect', cicadas emerge from under the ground every four years. This chutney is a delicacy in these parts. I have no expectation that many people will make this one, but you're at least curious, right?

Ingredients
1 cup cicadas (from a reputable source)
Oil (to deep fry)
1 tbsp lemon juice
1 tbsp salt
2-3 green peppers, sliced
1 tbsp ginger, sliced
1/2 onion, sliced

Heat oil in a pan and fry the cicadas until crisp. Remove and place on a paper towel for the oil to drain.
Toss the fried cicadas with salt and lemon juice to coat them evenly. (They can be eaten even now, paired with a cold beer.)

Mash the peppers, ginger, onions and fried cicadas together into a coarse paste. It will be a dry chutney.

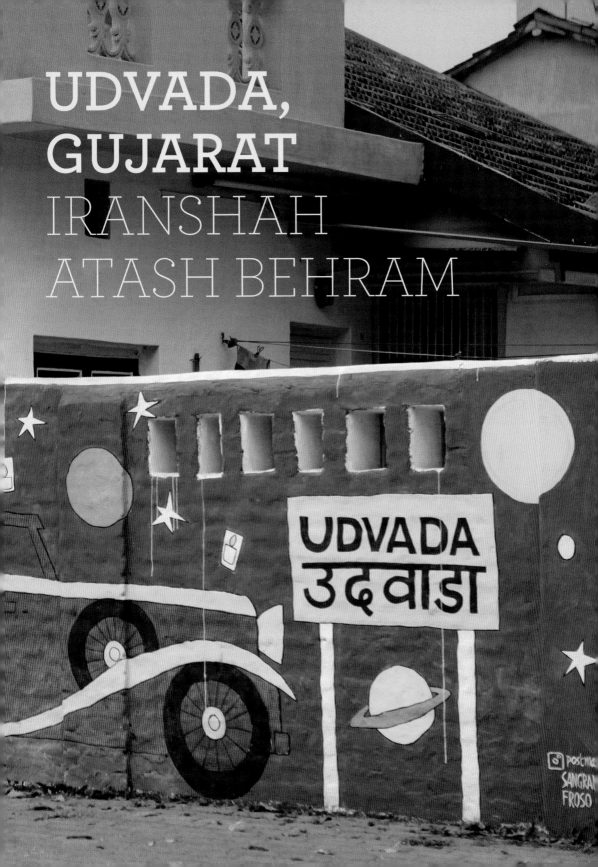

UDVADA, GUJARAT
IRANSHAH ATASH BEHRAM

UDVADA
उदवाडा

A different time and place. That's what we entered walking into Udvada, a small town on the coast of Gujarat that's become a rallying point for Parsi culture in India. Sun-baked streets, the rustic smell of sandalwood in the air and, for a town so small, a surprising amount of food around every corner.

The people of Udvada embody the resilience of their culture. A testament to the passage of time and a history that hasn't been all too fair. But in this town, you'll soon realize that the past itself can be a fickle thing. As old people are prone to forgetting, historical events themselves can get jumbled over time. The stories of legends, passed down through word-of-mouth, might not be in tune with the original tale. History is often dictated by the victor. The future, however, is yet to be tread.

The fire is a central element in both the Zoroastrian faith and Parsi cuisine. As a fireplace was once the fulcrum of a household, the Fire Temple or Iran Shah— said to be the oldest fire in India dating back to the time in Iran[6]—is the centre of this Parsi town. The name Iran Shah, king of Iran, signifies its ties for the Parsi community to their once true home. Thus, Udvada has become the centre of Parsi existence—past, present and future.

WHAT'S IN A BOWL OF MILK?

A Story

When the Zoroastrian travellers reached the shore of Sanjan, the king sent an envoy bearing a bowl filled to the brim with milk. This was his sneaky way of politely letting the newcomers know that there was no place for them in the city.

The Dastur, or high priest, responded by taking some sugar from his pocket and mixing it into the bowl of milk. His response: just as this sugar is sweet, we will enrich the community, but just as it dissolves into the milk, we too will merge with this community, not disrupt it.

Hearing that, the king laid down his terms. And if they had secret handshakes back then, I hope they did one to seal the deal.

Another Story

When the Zoroastrian travellers reached the shore of Sanjan, the king sent an envoy bearing a bowl filled to the brim with milk. This was his sneaky way of politely letting the newcomers know that there was no place for them in the city.

The Dastur, or high priest, responded by taking a ring off his finger and dropping it into the bowl of milk. His response: as this ring settles, we will settle at the bottom, but as this ring will always remain intact, so will our identities.

Hearing that, the king laid down his terms. And if they had secret handshakes back then, I hope they did one to seal the deal.

FROM THE DOORS OF PERSEPOLIS

It's hard to describe the benign outsider feeling that creeps up on us while walking the streets of this slow-paced town. Udvada is quite small, no more than a 20 minute walk from one end to the other, and is very much set in its ways—entry to the fire temple is forbidden, marriage between faiths are rare, and daily routines are a must.

When a new crew rolls into town, news spreads fast. We must have exchanged dozens of momentary glances with the residents as we wandered about with our cameras and Dictaphone—and with each look thought to ourselves: something is amiss, why does it feel like we don't belong? Weary and confused, we found our way to the Zoroastrian Museum.

The foundation of this community was laid long ago (time immemorial) when early nomads began to settle down in Iran—the region Persis.

By the sixth century BC, Cyrus the Great had united the people of Iran and established the first Persian empire. Despite its portrayal in *300*, the Persian empire was not the one-dimensional Hollywood foe. Cyrus is remembered until today as 'The Anointed of the Lord' for providing aid to the Jewish community when they were pitted against the Babylonian king Nebuchadnezzar II.

And from there, the empire expanded into a territory that would one day stretch from Eastern Europe to west of the Indus Valley, with trade spanning the entire hemisphere.

Philosophers, merchants and scholars flocked to this city and, in turn, the Zoroastrian faith influenced many other world religions. Darius I picked up where Cyrus left off, focusing on governance and construction to unify the territories—commissioning marvels like the great city of Persepolis (which, unfortunately, was destroyed when Darius III faced-off against Alexander the Great [7]).

But the tides began to change during sixth century AD when the Zoroastrian culture and faith was put at risk by Arab invasion. To preserve centuries of history and a faith as old as modern history itself, the community broke off, spreading into nearby lands. One particular group found themselves on the shores of the land of the 'Hinds'[8].

Today these Iranian descendants from the region once known as Persis are called Parsis. The people of Udvada have known each other for years. The houses that line the streets have stood here for decades. Theirs is a culture that has spanned centuries; it was all here before us and hopes to be here long after you and I are gone.

For them, for the Parsi community to survive into the future, they must first protect their past. And for that to happen, we must remain outsiders.

SOUL FOOD

Ervad Marzban Hathiram played host to us during Navroze, or the Parsi New Year. 'Ervad' is the title bestowed to a minor Zoroastrian priest, so this man was very much orthodox in faith, but a liberal at heart who gladly opened his doors to us and gave us a crash course in the esoteric and mystic Ilm-e-Kshnoom school of Zoroastrianism.

A twenty-seventh generation Parsi—with tapestry proudly hanging on his home walls to prove it— he moved here after life as a financial controller to practice his faith. Despite his sacrifice and devotion, he is still seen as an outsider by some in the community. Yet, he soldiers on.

His specialization: the Zoroastrian death ceremonies conducted in four parts—Baj, Afringan, Farokshi and, lastly, Stum in which food is an integral part of the process. However, it is not offered to any god or fire as you might assume. Instead, it is offered to the soul of the person who has passed.

To explain this, Marzban made savvy use of his accounting background coupled with ideas from Ilm-e-Kshnoom. Roughly 3500 years ago, the prophet Zarathustra was enlightened with the monotheistic idea of God, or Ahura Mazda ('Ahura' meaning 'Lord of Life' and 'Mazda', 'Omniscient'). This ideology laid the basis for Zoroastrianism where the entire cosmos comes into play. Ahura Mazda is in a zone where time and space are one. The Amesha Spirits—manifestations of Ahura Mazda's nature—are spread through this celestial medium as the cosmos, stars, sun and fire. Our souls began with Ahura Mazda as one, Ruvan. It is said that an imperfection was found within that soul, and thus the entire universe—known and unknown—was created by breaking these souls into smaller fragments to find and purify the imperfection.

The stars, suns, humans, animals, plants and rocks are those fragments—in each is Ruvan, a very, very small fraction.

And now, these souls are on the journey back to salvation, back to purity, back to being one with Ahura Mazda. But this salvation cannot be attained through one soul. These fragments must reach salvation together, and upon our death, the soul is reawakened to be judged by its *humata, hukhta, hvarshta*. (No, not *Hakuna matata*, although that did become the unofficial soundtrack for the trip.) Humata, hukhta, hvarshta are among the first Zoroastrian tenets a child is instilled with: good thoughts, good words and good deeds. Simply put, good thoughts without any action isn't enough. It's the culmination of the three in our lifetime that is our golden ticket to God.

What exactly is good? Well that's for Ahura Mazda to decide.

Think of it as a karmic accounts ledger. Chances are most of us are going to be seeing more debits than credits when we expire. Our souls are going to need quite the cleanse. The shock of those red accounts coupled with the attempt to purify them leaves the souls tired.

That's where Marzban steps in.

Ingredients such as wheat, rose, sandalwood, copper and milk are further along the cycle to salvation, and therefore have a better resonance with our souls compared to dead matter (or durian, which totally makes sense). Adhering to these specific ingredients and strict procedures, he cooks food to fuel these souls.

And, our morbid take, to welcome them back to humanity.

KHAATU-MEETHU-TEEKHO

'Birla, Tata, wah wah, yahan ka atta wah wah.'
Salman Khan in Judwaa

North of Iran Shah lies the Globe Hotel, one of the oldest, family-run institutions of Udvada. A third generation continues to cater to travelling Parsis with meals prepared over wood-fuelled fires, reminiscent of their origin in Iranian cuisine. Despite travelling over time and space, the sour of dry fruit, the spice of ginger and the savoury of saffron that became essential to Iranian cuisine through the country's trade networks (and placement along the Silk Road) can still be tasted in Parsi dishes today.[9]

The underlying principle of Parsi cuisine is *Khaatu-Meethu-Teekho* or sour-sweet-spicy, finding balance or harmony through these flavours.

Khaatu (sour): kokam, sugar cane vinegar, tamarind, lime, dry fruits (like berries)

Meethu (sweet): jaggery, palm sugar and dry fruits (like apricots)

Teekho (spicy): turmeric, red chilies, cumin, coriander, cardamom, nutmeg, mace, cinnamon etc.

But the 'authenticity' of the cuisine began to be affected during the resettlement of the Parsi communities in India. The staples of the Indian pantry, the local Gujarati food, the indoctrination of Portuguese influences from Goan cooks in Parsi households and even Anglo-Indian influences when Parsis relocated to Bombay to assist the Raj—all have combined to create Parsi classics such as Akuri, Berry Pulao, Dhansak and even Boi, a fried mullet, Udvada's rising star.[10]

ICE CREAM, YOU SCREAM

Vinod Bhai has got to be the coolest guy in Udvada. When we went to visit his backyard ice cream factory, we were surprised to find that he, much like Marzban, had a former life. In his case it was as an engineer, before he embarked on the quest to feed this town ice cream.

Why? Purely for the joy of it.

Two things set his ice cream apart. For one, he stills uses old school, hand-churning techniques. Depending on the season, fruit pulp like sitaphal or mango will be mixed with milk and jaggery and then churned to perfection with just ice and salt. The other is his transport system—a rickshaw with in-built refrigeration that he cruises around in, bringing delight with every bite to this sleepy town—jerry-rigged himself.

We'd been shadowing a Navjote ceremony (a Zoroastrian coming-of-age) that was taking place over the weekend. And if there's any celebration in Udvada, Vinod Bhai will be present. Between the three of us, we polished off three times the daily recommended serving of ice cream, paired with a side of raspberry soda.

And as we were preparing for a siesta, we found Vinod still proudly working, selling vegetables at the local market. You could see the guilt on our faces.

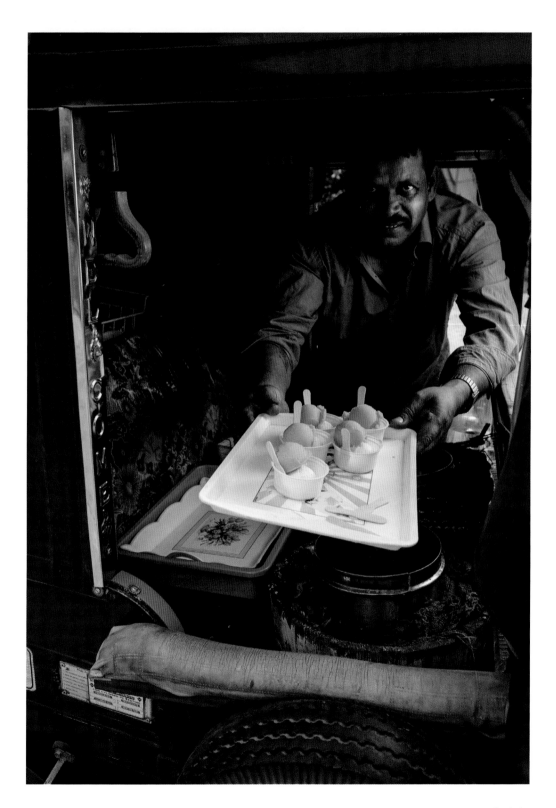

THE FIRE OF LIFE

A couple of days into our Udvada stay, we'd started to get a hold on the basics of Zoroastrianism, but one *burning* question remained: What's the importance of fire? And why can't we go see it?

(Sorry, two questions.)

So we knocked on Marzban's door once more.

The sun, stars and general cosmos are all extensions of Ahura Mazda, bestowing blessings upon humanity and aiding us on the path to salvation. And among them is the son of Ahura Mazda, *Asha*, or the Eternal Truth—manifested physically as fire. Just as fire physically purifies food, releases nutrition and transfers energy, it also purifies the mind and spirit, releases the true inner self and creates a connection between Ahura Mazda and us.

But talking about it didn't satiate our curiosity and since we weren't allowed to visit the temple itself, he took us directly to the source: a sandalwood 'factory'.

I say factory because, like most Indian companies, it had one mid-level manager whose job it was to boss people around and two workers who did all the manual labour: trimming the logs and setting them to bask in the sun where they hardened and turned red. The men's payment, aside from monetary, was a stipend of alcohol to help with their joint pain. But man, did one of them have a superb smile.

The majority of sandalwood logs, the kind used to fuel the fire of Iran Shah, come from Mysore—a lucrative supply chain given the high price of sandalwood. Before its price skyrocketed, whenever someone came to the fire to make a wish, they would offer sandalwood equal to their own weight, but now these scales have become more of a tourist attraction.

The reason for these strict doctrines is the magnitude of the fire that rests inside Iran Shah. In Zoroastrianism, there exist three grades of fire varying in source, purification power and purpose. The fire in Iran Shah is Atash Behram, the highest grade, born of sixteen fires. These sixteen are collected from in and around the community: the oven of the baker, the forge of the smith, the fire of death and even lightning.

The fire of lightning is probably not easy to source, but leaving this to its respective legend, the collection is just the start of this process followed by quite a robust purification ceremony.[11] And that in itself is a good enough reason to keep clumsy folk like us out—let alone the anxiety that we would face ourselves being inside.

From the earliest of nomads, fire has been the centre of the tribe. Warmth, light, protection—all very important, but even more significantly, fire allowed us to consume foods that we couldn't before, by destroying bacteria and unlocking nutritional value. Cooking was the first major advancement of the culinary world, and fire the reason behind the evolution of nomadic tribes into expansive civilizations.[12]

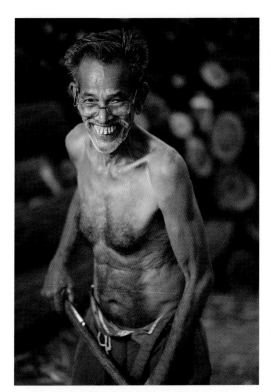

BOI, OH BOI!
(BOI NI MACCHI)
(Serves 4)

As the Parsi community settled on Gujarat's shores, nautical beings, such as the Boi in this recipe, became culinary staples.

Ingredients
2 tbsp salt
2 tbsp turmeric
2 tbsp red chilli powder
1 egg
3-4 tbsp oil, vegetable or mustard
4 whole boi or mullet, gutted and cleaned
1 lemon, quartered

Mix all the spices with the egg and then apply directly on to the fish.
Keep the marinated fish aside for 4-6 hours, covered and refrigerated.
Heat the oil in a pan and shallow-fry fish for 3-4 minutes on each side until it begins to brown.
Place on paper napkins to let the oil drain before serving hot with lemon.

PAPRA &
BAKHRA
(Serves 4)

Papra and Bakhra are two of the religious
dishes that are made specifically for the
Stum ceremony in the death rituals. For
us still living, they make great snacks.

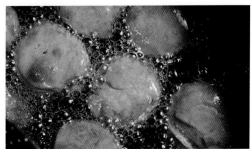

Papra

Ingredients
1 cup whole wheat flour
1 cup refined flour
¾ cup caster sugar
3 tbsp sesame seeds, roasted and ground
A pinch of salt
A pinch of caraway seeds, roasted and ground
A pinch of nutmeg powder
A pinch of cardamom powder
1 tbsp ghee
2 cups oil
Water, as needed

Mix all the dry ingredients together thoroughly.
Add the ghee and a little water at a time to knead the mixture into a dough.
Roll the dough out into cylinders roughly 2 cm in diameter and 8 cm long and cut each into 6 equal pieces. (Repeat with any remaining dough.)
Heat the oil in a pan over medium flame.
Roll the pieces of dough into flat discs around 6 cm across, keeping them on the thicker side.
Heat a heavy-bottomed pan and bake the discs, 2 minutes on each side, allowing them to partially cook.
Immediately after drop the discs into the oil, frying for another 3 minutes.
Take the papra out, drain the oil and let them cool before serving.

Bakhra

Ingredients
2 tbsp caraway seeds
2 cups whole wheat flour
¼ cup fine semolina
½ cup caster sugar
¼ tsp salt
½ tsp cardamom powder
½ tsp nutmeg powder
1 egg
1 tsp vanilla essence
1 tsp ghee
½ cup toddy, or palm wine
1 cup oil

Roast the caraway seeds in a pan over low heat until they start to brown and coarsely grind them.
Mix all the dry ingredients thoroughly. Make a well in the middle and plop the egg into it. And add the vanilla and ghee. Now add the toddy, 2 tablespoons at a time, and knead the dough.
Let it rest on a kitchen counter, covered overnight.
Roll out the dough into a large circle, roughly 1 cm thick. Use a circular cookie cutter, 2–3 cm in diameter, to cut out discs. Knead the remaining dough into a ball, roll it out and cut more discs. Repeat until you've used up all the dough.
Heat the oil in a pan over medium flame and deep-fry the discs for 3–4 minutes, flipped only a couples times. They should swell in size slightly, and are ready when lightly brown on the outside and thoroughly cooked on the inside.

AKURI
(Serves 2)

Akuri is the Parsi spin on scrambled eggs.

One ingredient in Parsi cooking that might seem difficult to procure is dhansak powder. Think garam masala, only leaning heavier on the coriander and cumin (2 spoons coriander : 1 spoon cumin) with the addition of red chilli powder.

This spice in usually available in two forms: dhansak powder, which is dry, and dhansak sambar, in which oil has already been added to the spice mix—giving the ingredients more time to bond and chat about their feelings.

Ingredients
1 tbsp oil (plus some to fry the onions)
1 onion, sliced thinly
3-4 green chilies
6 garlic cloves
1 tbsp ginger paste
1 tsp turmeric
1 tsp red chilli powder
1 tsp dhansak sambar
1 tsp coriander powder
1 tsp roasted cumin powder
2 tomatoes, pureed
Salt, to taste
4 eggs

Heat the oil in a pan and shallow-fry half of the onion until it browns and becomes crispy.
Mix the onion (raw and fried), chillies, garlic cloves and ginger paste in a blender.
Transfer the paste to the pan and fry it over medium heat, roughly 3-4 minutes.
Add the spices, tomatoes and salt.
Keep cooking until the tomatoes have darkened and the moisture has dried up.
Add the eggs directly into the pan with the paste, constantly stirring and mixing (or scrambling).
While the eggs are still slightly moist, after 3-4 minutes, remove from the heat and serve warm with toast.

KOLKATA, WEST BENGAL
MAGHEN DAVID SYNAGOGUE

Yellow ambassadors. Alleys of bustling commerce. Crowds of commuters. Relics of a colonial past. The streets of Kolkata are a maze of identities.

This city has long played host to an assortment of ethnic communities, from Armenians to Chinese. But the diversity that once formed the base of this cosmopolitan city has begun to dwindle.

No better example of this diversity exists than the red brick Renaissance masterpiece, Maghen David Synagogue, standing proud . . . yet empty, without a congregation inside. The community that surrounds it, the Baghdadi Jews of Kolkata, has gone from a few thousand to twenty.

But a spark of hope remains. Even though more souls rest within the Jewish cemetery, than are living outside it, the community's commitment to preserve its culture and faith has yet to falter.

Their memories linger along the roads, through the buildings and within the synagogues. Even though, at their highest, their numbers might have reached only a few thousand, there's no doubting the character that they have imparted to the city.

And these, their lasting legacies, will outlive us all.

NUMBERS

Straight from the airport, we met Ms A.M. Cohen, one of these twenty, in the most ominous of places, a Jewish cemetery. Not the most typical first stop in our journey, but an eerily apt one to explore the history of a culture in decline.

As we followed her through the tombs, she narrated the story of a man who now lay in front of us—Shalome Obadiah Ha-Cohen.

One.
The year is 1798. Syrian native Shalome Obadiah Ha-Cohen, thirty-five, arrives in Calcutta, the capital of British India, in search of trading opportunities. Before Shalome most Jews had only come seasonally or temporarily.

Known as 'Jewish Chief Merchant' he establishes a base in the city along the

13

Sephardic Jewish trade routes that have
continued since the early medieval period—
from Alexandria, Yemen, to Bombay,
Colombo, Calcutta, all the way to Rangoon,
Singapore, Hong Kong, Shanghai and
Jakarta.[14,15]

Gems, muslin, opium, furs, rose water,
Arabian horses, more gems . . . you name it,
he got it.

Thirty.
Shalome settles down in Aloo Gudam with his
family; a permanent enclave starts to develop
around them. Jews from Surat, Iran, Yemen
and neighbouring areas follow and the mix of
cultural, economic and religious connections
officially forms the Jewish Community of
Calcutta.[16]

Six hundred.
The late 1800s. Shalome has passed away and his son picks up the mantle. The Ezras, another prominent family, commissions some of the institutions that still stand today.

In the Park-Esplanade region, the community revolves around the girls' school near New Market and in Central Kolkata, around Esplanade Mansion and three synagogues— Beth El, Naveh Shalone and Maghen David.[17]

Each of these synagogues faces the direction of Jerusalem, connecting the congregation to their ancestral and spiritual homeland—even at the cost of urban planning (as with Beth El which has awkwardly turned away from the street).

The community continues to grow and assimilate into the Kolkata lifestyle slowly discarding its Arabic attire and Judeo-Arabic language in favour of local Raj-era styles and English. As much prosperity as

this community begot, even in this foreign land nothing came before faith—commercial ventures and caravans alike would halt during feasts and festivals.

Five thousand.
The community reaches its largest numbers during the Second World War as people fleeing Japanese persecution in Burma and Europe continue to pour into the Calcutta community.

Within the Jewish community, India gains a reputation as a country that does not discriminate against them. From army generals to high court judges to even the first Miss India, the Kolkata Jews became an indispensable part of Indian culture.[18]

Back to hundreds.
Even though during Partition, the community was largely left to its own devices, many land and business owners feared the uncertainty that Independence would bring and started

to leave the country for new opportunities. Australia and Canada, now open to immigrants, were two such destinations.

But perhaps the largest factor in this exit was the founding of the state in Israel in 1948. Indian Jews were well-versed in English and this new state needed them; many left, exchanging their Calcutta homes for tents.[19]

As a response to the decline, The Jewish Girls' School, which was established as an alternative to Christian schools, was opened to the public and today serves 1500 girls, many of whom are from other faiths.[20]

Twenty.
Today. Now. This moment. The number of people in the community stands in the twenties. Since the minimum number of males required for a congregation to take place at Maghen David is 10, the future of this community remains uncertain.

Ethno-religious is a term that's often used to describe the Jewish community—a community that is tied together not only by its faith or culture, but a combination of the two. The Baghdadi Jews of Kolkata illustrate this beautifully. Sephardic, Ashkenazi, conservative or orthodox, Ms Cohen believes that no matter which synagogue you walk into in any part of the world, it will be like home.

Shalome never returned to his homeland, choosing instead to live out his last days in Calcutta and be buried in the Jewish Cemetery he himself acquired. Two centuries later, Ms Cohen runs a daily routine through these institutions. Her morning begins with housekeeping at the cemetery, followed by administrative tasks at the Jewish Girls' School, and then a round at the synagogues to light the candles—all for the sake of preserving the future of their past.

If you ask her how she feels about the decline and the future for this community, Ms Cohen responds with a shrug and the Bengali saying: 'Jaa kaupalè lekha aachhè, sheyi haubè.'

What's written in your destiny is bound to happen.

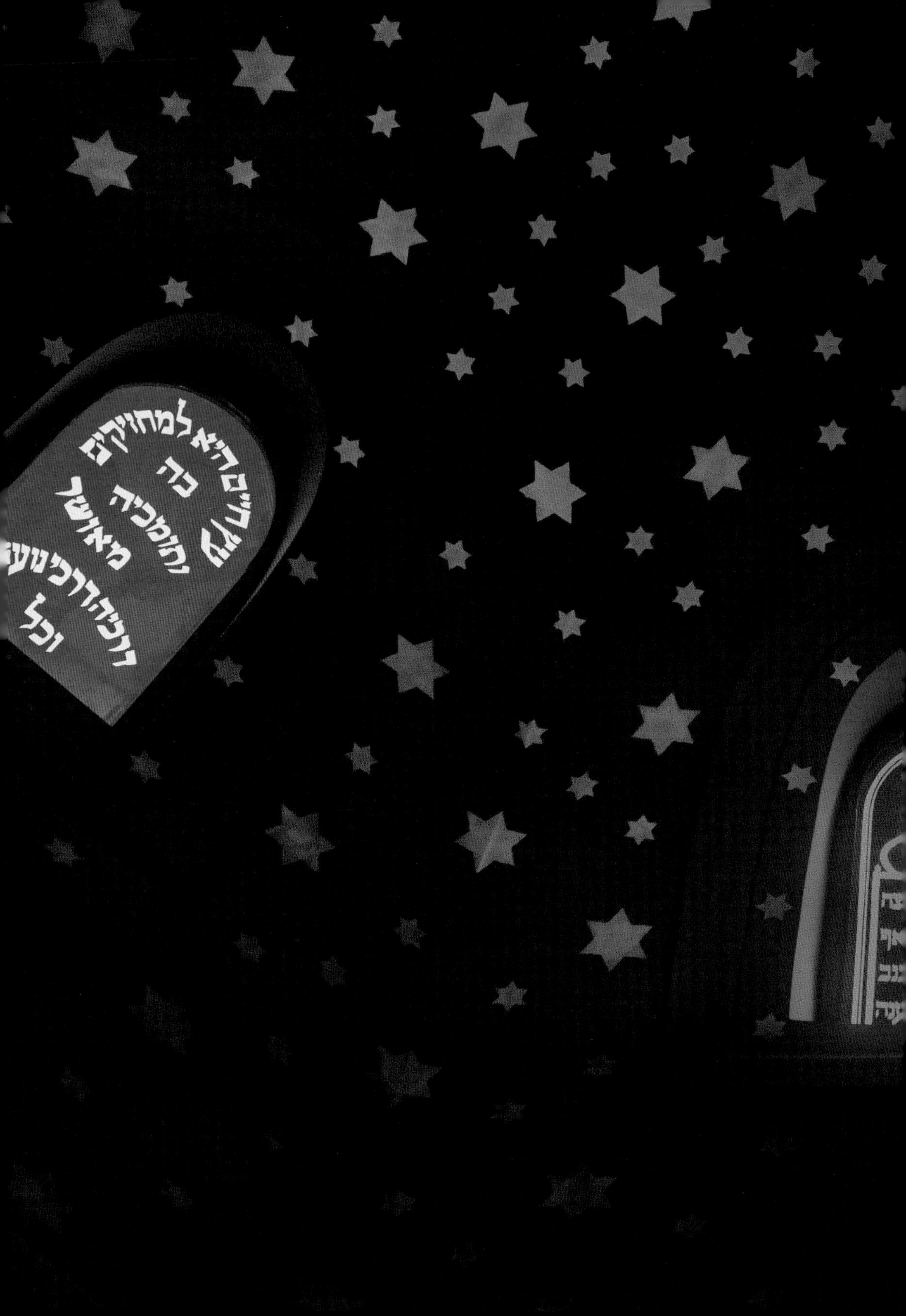
היא למחזיקים
בה
ותומכיה
מאושר
וכל

THE TEN COMMANDMENTS

I am the Lord thy God, thou shall not have any gods before me.

You shall not make for yourself an idol in the form of anything.

You shall not misuse the name of the Lord your God.

Remember the Sabbath day by keeping it holy.

Honour your father and your mother.

You shall not murder.

You shall not commit adultery.

You shall not steal.

You shall not give false testimony against your neighbour.

You shall not covet your neighbour's house, wife, or property.

MISS INDIA

This has absolutely nothing to do with anything Bhagwaan or Pakwaan, but Esther Victoria Abraham was one badass chick who highlights how ingrained individuals from the Jewish community became in India's culture and commerce.

At the age of seventeen, she left Calcutta and the Baghdadi Jewish community to train in a Parsi theatre company, eventually working her way to become the country's first Miss India in 1947–while pregnant with her fifth child. A scandal at the time (and, unfortunately, even today), this child was with a Shia Muslim.

With the stage name Pramila, she went on to star in over thirty films; followed by producing another sixteen, establishing herself as one of India's first major female producers. But despite leaving her community at a very young age, her faith and culture remained with her until the end.

When she passed away in 2006, one son recited Hebrew scriptures at Maghen David, while another son recited the Arabic equivalent.

A GOAN BAKERY IN KOLKATA THAT MAKES DOUGHNUTS FOR THE JEWISH COMMUNITY

Sometimes a title is enough.

KOLKATA KOSHER

At the gates of Maghen David the first person to greet you will be the Muslim caretaker—a generation-spanning role—with a *kippah* in his hands, waiting to adorn your head.

Flower Silliman, another cultural crusader of this community, tells us that the Jewish and Muslim communities have kept close ties since the early Baghdadi traders moved in—one of their first cultural exchanges would have taken place in the Jewish kitchens.

In the first five books of the Torah, guidelines are laid out to define what is kosher, meaning allowed or appropriate, under this tradition. Some of the kosher items are: creatures that both chews its cud and has split hooves (barring animals like pigs, hares and camels) and fish that have both fins and scales (but no shellfish). However, creepy, crawly, flying things, for the most part, are not kosher.

Regulations exist for the preparation and consumption of food as well. It's forbidden to eat meat and dairy in the same meal. The slaughtering of an animal has to be quick, painless and void of any blood in the resulting meat—which led to a strict ritual slaughtering *comparable* to halal.[21] Since pork is not kosher, a belief shared in Islam, Muslim chefs were often hired to run Jewish kitchens—often split into two sides, meat and dairy.

But this would be only one of the major influences to their Iraqi diet.

Calcutta had long been a thriving port of trade by the time the Jews settled down. Here they got access to local ingredients—new spices and herbs (chillies, ginger, coriander) and tropical produce (tamarind, pumpkin, coconut).

(An etymological tangent: The word 'tamarind'–imli–actually comes from the Arabic 'tamr hindi' or 'Indian date'.[22])

Kosher fish was easier to procure and became a major source of protein in the evolving diet. Coconut milk allowed the Baghdadi Jews to circumvent the milk 'n' meat kosher rule–a hack learnt from the Cochin Jews of the south. After simmering in Calcutta, their cuisine became spicier and tangier; their once soupy stews slowly became more like curries.[23,24,25]

Flower herself is quite the interesting specimen–born and raised in Kolkata, she travelled back to Jerusalem briefly to open an Indian restaurant, Maharaja. But eventually returned to Kolkata.

India is her true home and she takes pride in the fact that she's never felt prejudice here as a Jew. And thus, she will play her part in keeping the flicker of this community alive through tracking their food.

BREAKING BREAD
And on the seventh day, God rested.

For observant Jews, this day is known as Shabbat and is a day of rest and reflection. Shabbat begins at nightfall on Friday (the Jewish day begins at sunset) and continues until nightfall on Saturday.

Saturdays are a day to spend time with family and abstain from work—driven from Halakha or Jewish law where thirty-nine activities ranging from ploughing to cooking to lighting a fire are prohibited. It's because of this that the day prior, Friday, becomes a celebration or the welcoming of Shabbat and thus, a night to feast.[26]

Flower's Shabbat schedule is reminiscent of an older time, when the Jewish community of Kolkata was larger.

Friday

After the lighting of candles and the evening service at the synagogue, the meal begins with breaking bread (challah) dipped in salt while reciting the Kiddush over a cup of wine. The bread represents food, manna that God provided during the dessert exodus, and the salt, a common mineral from the historical lands, a covenant with God.[27]

The first course is Aloo Makallah with Hilbe, Zalata (cucumber salad), with Mahashas (stuffed vegetables) and roast chicken. It is often followed by simple pulao eaten with a curried dish of meat, like fish or chicken in Chitanee, a sweet and sour gravy, or Bamia Khatta, a lighter curry with okra or beets that gets its name from its sour taste. Or, in keeping with Baghdadi cuisine, Kubba which is a rice dumpling stuffed with meat and cooked in a stew.

Saturday

Hamim (meaning 'hot') is an ingenious dish that helped circumvent the Shabbat restrictions while providing a warm meal on Saturday morning. Slowly cooked over the dying embers through the night, this one pot wonder consists of a whole hen stuffed with rice and innards, then immersed into a stew of more chicken pieces, vegetables and rice, and then to top it off: rice dumplings and eggs.

After a night of steamy romance, the hamim is separated into three distinct dishes: Hashwa (the stuffed hen), Shorba (the stew) and Hakaka (the crispy brown crust along the bottom). This, along with leftovers, is converted into salads and appetizers and served as the Shabbat then comes to an end.[28]

ALOO MAKALLAH WITH HILBEH

(Serves 4)

This dish best represents the influence of Kolkata on the cuisine the Baghdadi Jews brought with them.

Aloo, the Hindi word for potato, meets Makallah, Arabic for fried. A dish that's reminiscent of the Bengali aloo bhaja, but has a twist—it uses whole, fried potatoes. It's served with Hilbeh, a green chutney from Yemen but with the addition of local produce such as ginger, coriander and chilies.

The trick to getting these potatoes perfect is twofold. First, you ideally need to procure 3-4 month old potatoes that haven't been in cold storage and are meant for fries/crisps. Second, the double frying of the potatoes is what give them the extra crunchy exterior.

The following recipes have been inspired from Flower Silliman's *Three Cups of Flower*.

Aloo Makallah

Ingredients
8 whole potatoes, slightly larger than an egg, peeled
1 tbsp salt
1 tsp turmeric
Oil, depending on pot size
Water, depending on pot size

Bring a large saucepan with enough water to cover the potatoes to a boil, adding the salt and turmeric.
Place the potatoes in the saucepan—the bubbles will die down. When the water begins to boil again, immediately drain and cool.
Heat a deep pan with enough oil to cover the potatoes over medium flame and fry the potatoes until they develop a yellow crust.
Remove the pan from heat, allowing the potatoes to cool in the oil.
Prick each potato all around with a fork 3-4 times.
Around an hour before you are ready to serve, reheat the oil and potatoes over medium flame, allowing the potatoes to slowly develop their crunchy outer layer.
With 20 minutes to go, turn the flame up to high to get them nice and brown.
Drain and serve hot with Hilbeh.

Hilbeh

Ingredients
1 tbsp fenugreek seeds
¾ cup cold water
½ cup coriander leaves
½ tbsp ginger paste
½ tbsp garlic paste
2-3 green chilies
2 tbsp lemon juice
1 tsp salt

Soak the fenugreek seeds overnight.
Blend all the other ingredients together, adding the fenugreek seeds only at the end to avoid a slimy texture.
The remaining paste should be thick enough to lather on the potatoes at your discretion. The hilbeh will thicken over time due to the fenugreek seeds.
Serve chilled.

CUCUMBER ZALATA

(Serves 2)

Also common in the Baghdadi Jewish pantry were pickled items such as this quick-pickled cucumber.

Ingredients
2-3 seedless cucumbers, peeled
and thinly sliced
½ tbsp salt
1tsp chopped green chilies
1tbsp sugar
½ tbsp chopped ginger
½ tbsp chopped garlic
2 tbsp chopped mint
¾ cup cider vinegar
½ cup water

Salt the cucumber generously and let it stand
for one hour so that the cucumber can release
the water. After one hour, drain the excess
water.
Combine the chillies, sugar, ginger, garlic and
mint. Add the cucumber to the mix when ready.
Bring the vinegar to a boil and pour over the
cucumber mixture. Add enough water to cover
all the ingredients.
Allow to cool and store tightly sealed in the
fridge for up to a week.

MAHASHAS
(Serves 4)

Mahashas are one of the dishes
served during the Shabbat.

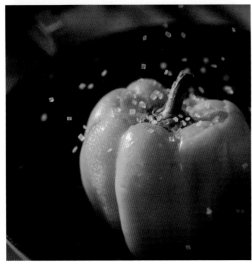

Ingredients
4 tbsp oil
½ yellow onion, diced
1tbsp ginger, chopped
1 tbsp garlic, chopped
1 cup chicken mince
¾ cup rice
1 tsp salt
2 tbsp sugar
8-10 pieces of the following: whole tomatoes, green or red capsicum, large chilli peppers
1 tbsp lemon juice
2 tbsp mint leaves, chopped
2 tbsp tamarind liquid
Water, as needed

Heat 2 tablespoons of the oil in a pan and sauté the onions until they begin to soften. Add the garlic and ginger and fry until they brown.
Mix in the mince and let it release its water for 3-4 minutes.
Just as the chicken is beginning to brown, add the rice, salt, 1 tablespoon sugar and add about ½ cup water. Let it simmer until the rice is partially cooked (10-15 minutes).
Meanwhile, core the tomatoes, capsicum, or peppers by slicing the top, using a spoon to remove any pulp and seeds. Do not discard the tops.
When the rice is ready, remove from heat and add the lemon juice and 1 tablespoon mint.
Fill the cored vegetables approximately ¾ of the way and place the lids back on top.
Heat the remaining 2 tablespoons of oil in a large pan over medium flame. Place the stuffed vegetables evenly spaced inside.
Add 1 tablespoon sugar, a pinch of salt, the tamarind liquid and the remaining mint leaves.
Cover and cook for 25-30 minutes until the vegetables have softened and the rice is cooked through, adding water as necessary to prevent sticking.

CHITANEE
(Serves 4)

Ingredients
2 tbsp oil
3-4 yellow onions, diced finely
1 tbsp ginger paste
1 tbsp garlic paste
2-3 red chillies, chopped
2 tsp coriander powder
2 tsp cumin powder
4 tomatoes, pureed
3 tbsp tamarind liquid
6-8 pieces of chicken (thigh, drum, or wings)
2 tsp salt
2 tsp sugar
Water, as needed
Lemon juice as needed

Heat the oil in a pan and sauté the onions, adding the garlic, ginger and chillies once they start to brown.
Next, add the cumin and coriander powders.
When the spices become fragrant, but haven't yet browned, add the tomatoes and tamarind liquid with the salt and sugar.
As the mixture thickens into a paste-like consistency, add ¾ cup water.
Once the gravy comes to a boil, add the chicken and simmer, covered, until the chicken is cooked through, about 10–15 minutes.
Remove the lid and allow some of the moisture to evaporate so that the gravy can thicken.
Squeeze a lemon on top and serve hot with rice.

PURI, ODISHA
SHREE JAGANNATH TEMPLE

Walking into Jagannath Temple is a lot like walking into the magical universe of Disney World.

There's Bada Danda or the grand road that leads you into the temple complex, with hawkers and hotels lined on either side. In Anandabazar, you can witness the preparation of enough food to feed the town; then in the market enough treats to put you in a food coma. Then there's *Bath Town* where Jagannath is showered and Swargadwara, the 'graveyard', where the old murtis are laid to rest. And finally, the main castle in the middle of it all, Garbhagriha, where Jagannath and his entourage await your visit.

The anticipation of bhog rivals that of waiting to take a selfie with your favourite character. The devotees' dedication to these idols is no different from Mickey fan boys teetering on the cusp of a cult. And much like how towns and tourism will develop around any theme park, Puri is no different. But while the enthusiasm for your favourite superhero might fade with time, in Jagannath, these *Mahan*-fans are loyal until the end.

MAN, GOD OR CELEB?

Jagannath had actually welcomed us to his home with a fair bit of bureaucracy. Turns out, although we'd been assured otherwise, photography within the complex was strictly forbidden. So it required a bit of greasing and *jugaad* to pull this chapter off.

That's where Haribol, one of the complex's resident priests, came in offering sage advice: (Paraphrasing) Pretend you are from Kolkata instead of Delhi or 'mainland India'. Apparently some people there don't like folk like us. (The humour in this statement is only exacerbated when you understand that I— Varud Gupta—already have enough trouble pronouncing the name of this book correctly.)

But moving on . . . Haribol was an insider. And it was within the folds of his dhoti that we smuggled in our phones and made a beeline straight for Jagannath.

At first glance Jagannath—tall, dark and handsome—comes across as quite the celebrity; big worldly eyes, adoring fans, syndication across Hindu, Jain and Buddhist texts, never without an entourage.

As we stood amongst those devoted fans in the hall, Haribol gave us the tour. There're Subhadra and Balabhadra, his siblings; Garuda, his ride; Jaya and Vijaya, the security team; and Sudarshan, the spinning chakra (for which there is no good analogy). Because the idol of the temple is so large—sandalwood cut from a golden axe—the Lord even has a 'stunt double' that makes appearances or take showers on his behalf.

In Hindu faith Jagannath, 'Lord of the Universe', is an incarnation of Vishnu, like Krishna, born in the period known as Kali Yuga. But outside of the Hindu pantheon, the origins of Jagannath are a mystery.[29] As Dr Abhaya Naik explains, that's perfectly fine for as you begin to chip away the sandalwood, you'll find a man that represents nothing more than a common being.

In the temple, Jagannath's day begins with routine. A timetable of tasks from brushing and showering to eating and planned relaxation. His idol will change outfits regularly according to venue and utility. And then there's the Chhappan Bhog or Mahaprasad to get him through the day: his daily diet of six meals composed of fifty-six dishes. Interestingly, it is his entourage that is offered Bhog first; after all, the ones around you who support you should be cared for first and foremost. Some of his rituals are oddly reminiscent of the banality of modern life such as occasional dietary restrictions or even catching a fever. Since Jagannath gets 'married' on a yearly basis, the priests at this temple don't practice abstinence and have lives and families outside the complex.

Jagannath condones the millennial motto: Work hard, play hard. Since he didn't have Netflix to unwind at night, Geeta Govinda, his favourite song about the relationship between Krishna and Radha, would be performed. During the summer months, he is carried on a twenty-one-day lake cruise vacation.

It's a common feature of our rising generation to become disenchanted with the traditions and ceremonies that often surround religion. And while some might escape logic, before the time of Facebook, how else could a society unify behind their values and lifestyle?

That's the true significance of Jagannath, a God no different from you or me.

LOST IN
TRANSLATION

A short drive from Puri, a crew of three—Varud, Devang and Toni—travel to a nearby UNESCO site.

Guide: (In a highly pronounced Indian American accent) The Konark sun temple was built in the thirteenth century and is famous for the *aero tic* engravings along the walls.

Varud: *Aero tic*? What's that?

Guide: *Aero tic* . . . How do I explain Aero tic?

Varud: Is it a word in Sanskrit?

Guide: No, *aero tic*, it's an English word.

Varud: *Aero tic*, I'm so confused.

Devang: Bro. He's saying erotic.

Varud: No he's not, pagal . . .

Varud pauses, his gaze upon the walls.

Varud: What the—

End scene.

It's completely normal to be surprised for a good 30 minutes or so into your tour of the Konark sun temple that there are erotic engravings all over these walls. Since I can't describe the motifs in detail, just think of your wildest fantasies—the lucky people along the walls are living them out.[30]

As our guide told us, the reason behind the engravings was that during the Ganga dynasty, a time filled a decent amount of bloodshed, Kalinga's (today Odisha-ish) population was hitting an all-time low.[31] So King Narasimha Deva, clearly an underrated genius, decided that while the temple would be *erected* in honour of Surya, there would be educational depictions along its walls to *stimulate* the community. In this ancient example of censorship, the depictions at the lower heights of the wall would be for children with simple animal designs to keep them occupied. The middle tiers would be for the working classes, primarily sexual in nature, but not without other lessons for the common household. And the upper tiers would depict religious aspects and traditions.

War was something that Kalinga had become all too familiar with at this point in time. Long before Narasimha built the sun temple there was another infamous ruler who changed the face of Odisha's landscape.

Asoka was one of the first movies to make me (Varud) cry. Towards the end of the movie, SRK cheers his men on to the battlefields of Kalinga. As the night passes, he finds his lady love, Kareena Kapoor, holding the body of the future of king of Kalinga–a child he had met earlier when… sorry, spoiler alert?

These events, although fictionalized, are not so removed from reality.

In 260 BCE, King Ashoka did invade Kalinga. According to his own accounts, this battle was so devastating that it inspired his journey to Buddhism.[32] Kalinga, which had before enjoyed a degree of independence, became an integral part of subsequent Indian dynasties until it was finally absorbed into the Mughal empire and thereafter the British Raj. Along the way, the territory came to be known as Odisha.[33]

During British occupation, the Odia people didn't submit willingly. Through revolt and rebellion, they became a difficult territory for the British to manage. As a consequence, Odia regions were divided into neighbouring territories–a large portion joining Bengal.[34] (Local rumour has it that the infamous rasgulla and other Bengali dishes might be of Odia origin, as richer Bengali households often employed Brahmin cooks from here.) But the culture of Orissa persisted and it became the first language-based province in 1936.[35] Today, in a state that is still 2/5 classified as tribal, relics of an ancient tradition live on.[36]

In short: in the pre-Playboy days, any trick is worth it if it's helping a population in decline.

GREEN IS THE NEW BLACK

One of our favourite practices around Mahaprasad was the idea of setting aside caste, race, or wealth to eat together from one plate that everyone shared. The problem on the other hand is when sharing with other foodies, certain people might eat all the good things first.

And that's how we found ourselves—a priest, a cook and three Delhiites—in the Ram Mandir eating the Chhappan Bhog.

All of the ingredients for these fifty-six dishes are local. Not in the trendy farm-to-table way; local such that only produce native to India is used—no tomatoes (aka vilayati baigan), no potatoes (vilayati aloo) and no green chillies. On top of which, to our dismay, garlic and onions are also considered non-veg.
But digging into the famous besar, it was love-at-first-bite. How?

Leaving the food market, the cook took us to the kitchen corner where an estimated 10,000-plus people—more during special occasions—are served daily. Behind the closed doors, he said, 752 stoves burn through the day with 9 handis cooking on each and 1000 cooks either operating the stoves or preparing the one-pot wonders. The cook was initially wary of giving us an in-depth look at the preparations and recipes, but a round of paan (along with our charming personalities) got the ball rolling.

Black pepper was the first secret. Even before India became a colony, black pepper was highly prized in the spice trade, leading to the Dutch phrase 'pepper expensive'. It was one of the commodities that pushed the Portuguese to seek a faster sea-route to India, bringing Vasco de Gama to our eastern shores in 1498.[37] Its ubiquity in India was eventually replaced by the hotter chillies, but not in Jagannath's kitchen. Along with this, most dishes are built from a spice blend of panch phoran—black mustard, nigella seeds (kalonji), fenugreek, cumin and fennel seeds. Asafoetida or hing substitutes the missing pungency from garlic or onions.

Another reason behind the taste is the use of the clay pots, one stacked on top of the other over a roaring fire keeps the taste and aromas trapped. That and the liberal use of jaggery and ghee.

A few bites more, and then, *Yummy Belly Syndrome* hits.

Yummy Belly Syndrome
noun

1. The soporific effect of gluttonous food consumption, sometimes associated with euphoric or giddy behaviour
'After eating at the Bhog Mandapa, Devang, Varud and Toni experienced Yummy Belly Syndrome and passed out.'

Synonyms: food coma
Origin: Varud's cousin Vidur

A 56-COURSE DAY

Mahaprasad is considered so auspicious by some, that after it has been offered to Jagannath, the same prasad can then be offered to other gods and goddesses.

Gopal Ballav Bhog is the breakfast that begins at 9 a.m. after Jagannath changes and showers. They say this meal is supposed to be light but with dishes such as Peda, Kora, Dahi and assorted fruits, the feast has already begun. Only an hour after this, the morning offering or Sakala Dhupa starts. Dishes resembling a proper meal are included such as Kanika, Khechudi and Enduri.

Bhog Mandapa is primarily cooked for the consumption of the pilgrims or local population, and thus, this is one of the biggest offerings. Everything from Masala and Meetha Daals, assorted Chawals, Saag and Subjis, Chutneys and desserts like Payas or Rabri.

This is followed by Madhyam Bhog, Jagannath's mid-day meal which is kind of like his snack break before taking rest for the day.

Then there's Sandhya Bhog around 7 p.m. which is the evening tiffin for the deities. But we still aren't finished. The day ends with Badasimhar Dhoop in which just a few items are offered, including pure ghee in a silver container.[38]

BESAR
(Serves 4)

We're going to cook this like they do in the temple—a one-pot dish—as best we can at home. The main difference in the temple method is that ghee is only added at the end, due to its ability to break traditional clay pots.

Ingredients

1 cup black lentils
2 tbsp ghee (plus extra to fry)
2 tbsp mustard seeds
1 tbsp coriander powder
1 tbsp cumin
1 tsp fenugreek leaves
1 tsp nigella seeds
1 tsp fennel seeds
1 tsp black pepper
1 cup pumpkin, cut into 2 cm cubes
1 cup taro, cut into 2 cm cubes
1 cup green banana, sliced to 1 cm pieces
1 tsp turmeric
1 tbsp jaggery
Salt to taste
1 tbsp ginger paste
½ cup freshly grated coconut

Subji

Blend the mustard seeds into a paste with 1-2 tablespoons of water as necessary.

In a second pan, heat the 2 tablespoons of ghee over medium flame.

Add the coriander powder, cumin, fenugreek, nigella, black pepper and fennel seeds; toast lightly.

Add the chopped vegetables and cook for 3-4 minutes, till the water begins to let out.

Add the mustard paste, turmeric, salt, jaggery and ginger paste.

Add 1 cup water. Once the mixture comes to a boil, cover the pan and let it simmer until the vegetables are cooked through, 15-20 minutes. The water should be mainly gone, with just a little dry gravy.

Top with the fried badi and some more ghee (optional) to embrace the temple taste, and the grated coconut.

Mix and let it cook for 2-3 minutes more before serving hot with rice.

Dal Badi

Soak the lentils overnight.

Drain the water from lentils and transfer them to a blender. Keep adding 2-4 tablespoons of water as necessary to get a wet paste-like consistency.

Heat ghee in a pan over medium flame. Drop little globules, 2-3 cm in size, into the pan.

Fry for 3-4 minutes, until they are brown. Then remove and set aside on a paper towel to drain the excess oil.

POTOL PANEER
(Serves 4)

Potol (pointed gourd or parwal) is one of the items that is cooked regularly in the kitchens of Jagannath. But we found a variation of the dish at one of the neighbouring temples, where paneer was being added. The following is the traditional recipe with a twist fit for celebrations.

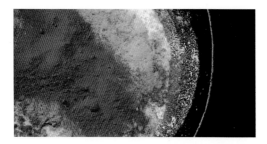

Ingredients

2 tbsp ghee (plus extra to fry)
1 cup pointed gourd, sliced lengthwise into 3-4 pieces
200 grams paneer, cut into thick cubes
1 tbsp curry powder
1 tbsp cumin
1 tbsp ground black pepper
1 tbsp coriander powder
1 tbsp fenugreek
1 tbsp ginger paste
½ cup cashews, ground into a paste
1 tbsp red chilli powder
1 tsp green cardamom
1 tsp turmeric powder
1 tsp cinnamon powder
1 tbsp condensed milk
1 tbsp fresh cream
1 tsp milk powder
½ cup leftover rice water
Salt to taste

Heat the ghee in a wok over medium flame, then fry the gourd, 4–5 minutes, until the skin starts to brown. Drain on to paper towels.
Next fry the paneer in ghee over medium heat for 4-5 minutes, until it starts to brown.
Add 2 tablespoons of ghee into a pan over medium heat. Once warm, add the curry, cumin, black pepper, coriander, fenugreek, ginger paste and the cashew paste.
Once the spices start to brown, add the red chilli, cardamom, turmeric, cinnamon powder, condensed milk, cream, milk powder and the rice water.
Cook for 4-5 minutes until the gravy begins to thicken and the moisture evaporates. The resulting masala will have a fair amount of liquid gravy. Add salt to taste and remove from heat.
In a separate pan, warm the gourd and the paneer and then slowly spoon back in the masala gravy.
Serve hot with Besar and rice.

MALPUA
(Serves 4)

Malpua highlights the idea that mahaprasad is meant to be shared. Primarily, because it's hard to finish these bad boys by yourself.

Ingredients

Batter
1 cup refined flour
½ cup semolina
½ cup sugar
½ tsp ground black pepper
1 tsp fennel seeds
1 cup milk
Ghee (to deep fry)

Jaggery Syrup
1 cup jaggery
3-4 tbsp milk
½ tsp green cardamom powder

Mix the dry batter ingredients together.
Slowly add the milk, whisking constantly to break any lumps. The batter should have a medium-wet consistency. Set aside for 30 minutes.
Heat a pan over a low flame. Add the jaggery and allow it to melt before slowly spooning in the milk. Cook the mixture for 1–2 minutes then add the cardamom powder.
Cook the syrup, 2–3 minutes more, until it just starts to reach a sticky consistency. Set aside.
Heat ghee in a pan over a medium flame.
Spoon a ladleful of the batter into the pan as evenly as possible.
Fry for 1 minute before flipping and repeating. The batter should start to puff up and brown on both sides.
Remove the malpua from the heat and soak in the jaggery syrup for 10 minutes.
Drain and serve!

SPITI, HIMACHAL PRADESH

KYE GOMPA

IT'S 6 A.M.
All you want to do is sleep.

Yesterday concluded the first sixteen-hour leg of the journey north on an overnight bus. And today there's another ten.

But sleep isn't an option. The rocky road jolts you awake as you jostle your way over the Rohtang Pass into Spiti valley. The roller coaster of a Tempo Traveller is adorned with paraphernalia: a picture of the jolly Dalai Lama clapping to the music, the chant Om Mane Padme Hum endlessly spinning on the dashboard, and Buddhist idols glaring back at you from where they've been stuck on the window.

Not to mention, the classic Bollywood songs of the 1980s that the driver is playing to 'enliven' the ambience. The lyrics are now trapped in your head—*Pehla nasha, pehla khumaar*—repeating as you exit the vehicle for a restroom break.

And then, it finally hits you: tumbling waterfalls; autumn yellows speckled through the trees; cocoa cliffs line the horizons with floral notes of pink; boulders sprawled out, relaxing in the sun.

All this in a desert. A desert far from the India you know where the locals are more social than South Delhiites, where bikers with decadent handlebar moustaches rule the roads, where at every rest stop you'll find a humble dhaba paired with a small Buddhist temple, and where Salman Khan is unanimously popular.

You close your eyes as you zip up your pants. The air effortlessly fills your lungs.

And as you open them, the ten hours have breezed away, and in front of you lies Kye Gompa, a Tibetan monastery nestled away in the valley. Welcome to the Dalai Lama's (alleged) favourite crib.

GAMES OF THRONES

If India had its own *Game of Thrones* series, Kye Gompa would be King's Landing. Just imagine it: Tyrion in breakout dance sequences, Cersei the melodramatic mother-in-law and Mallika Dua as Brienne of Tarth taking everyone's case. (Balaji call us anytime to further discuss).

It's not only the striking solitude of Kye Gompa that brings to mind these fictional worlds. Turns out, Spiti still has a king: Nono, who's a fan of classic Western movies like The Magnificent Seven (OG) and *Butch Cassidy and the Sundance Kid*.

His name isn't actually Nono—it's Sonam Angdui—but that is the title that everyone in town uses, a title that comes from the time of the British Empire.

CUE FLASHBACK.

The history of Kye Gompa is filled with potentials and maybes. The reason for this confusion is that Spiti was home to frequent attacks by Mongols (during the seventeenth century), destruction (during the Ladakh and Kullu wars in 1820), a fire (in the 1840s), invasions (by the Dogra and Sikh armies separately in 1841) and finally an earthquake (in 1975).[39]

But apart from this series of unfortunate events, Nono attributes the current state of affairs in Spiti to an isolated history. This began to first change during the British Era, when even isolated areas were made into governing posts under British supremacy. Spiti was once associated with the Ladakhi structure—which is where the title Nono, meaning little brother came from.
Today, Nono is only a title, but he continues

to push Spiti into the modern age—aiming to bring the Tibetan and Indian cultures together. This task might seem easy given that Spiti is a homogenous community across faith (Buddhism), language (Spitian) and lifestyle (self-sustaining farms). But external influences have started to change that self-contained peace: cash crops, tourism and the need for sustainable waste disposal.

That's enough chit-chat. It's time to head into Kye Gompa itself, where a night's stay in October makes one thing clear:

Winter is coming.

A SPITIAN CRASH COURSE

Hello = **Juley**

Spiti = **Peeti**

Wanna grab some Chaang (a drink) with me? = **Kno champo chaang thonga?**

Where's the bathroom? = **Knola chap sang thang du dogarak?**

All good? = **Chuk yotha?**

All good = **Nyo kamzang yu.**

Kuch Kuch Hota Hai = **Chitong chitong ta.**

Where are you going? = **Kala dona?**

Water = **Chu.**

Food = **Thopcha.**

What are you cooking? = **Thopcha chi yotha?**

Goodbye = **Juley**

NEW KID
ON THE
BLOCK

We finally managed to swap out the tunes
of the Golden Era of Bollywood with the
echoed hums of Om Mane Padme Hum that
have made a home for themselves in the
Spiti Valley. In the two nights we spent in Kye
Gompa, we came to realize that Buddhism is
more than a faith in Spiti, it's a way of life.

Buddhism was born roughly 2500 years ago when Siddhartha Gautama or Shakyamuni Buddha, a prince, met a dying man outside his palace walls and was smacked in the face by the certainty of death. In search of happiness and an end to suffering, he embarked on a pilgrimage initially through an ascetic lifestyle, before he settled under a banyan tree on the banks of River Niranjana.[40]

We can never know what truly happened in those hours and days that followed, when Siddhartha's meditation led him to attain Bodhi, or enlightenment, around the middle way of moderation. But suffice it to say that his, and our, world was about to change. Thanks to Indian scholars, such as Nagarjuna, and rulers like Ashoka, Buddhism travelled from India to other parts of the world—Japan, Tibet, South East Asia and China. And as it spread, it developed local flavours.

In Tibet's isolation, Buddhism found a stronghold of solace and thrived. TsongKhaPa, or Je Rinpoche, in the fourteenth century, collected and studied texts across the region aiming to bring together all these schools of thought. The result was a slight reformation: Gelug, the school of thought practiced in Kye Gompa.

Gelug is a 'system of virtue' with an emphasis on intellectual study—monks travel to south India to obtain doctorates in Buddhist philosophy, where they are also encouraged to debate any schisms in belief.

Think of Gelug Buddhism as the nerdy kid at school. In reality, and stemming from experience, that kid is likely to spend his high school days at the bottom of the food chain. But when it comes to Gelug, this nerd was voted class king—even Tenzin Gyatso, the current Dalai Lama, is a practitioner.[41]

A DAY AS A CHILD MONK

A unique quirk of Kye Gompa is the soon-to-be monks who also call this place home. When a boy first joins the monastery in line with Gelug practice, he is immediately placed into a rigorous routine to study Buddhist ideals, languages (including the ancient Bodhi), mathematics, science and the arts.

Their daily schedule might be something like this:

6 a.m.: Wake up and study languages (Bodhi, Hindi and English)
8.30 a.m.: Breakfast
10 a.m.: Head to school to study (mathematics, science and the arts)
12.30 p.m.: Lunch and then return to school
4 p.m.: School homework
5.30 p.m.: Dinner
6 p.m.: Free time (football, cricket or TV)
7 p.m.: Continued studies of Bodhi and school homework
9.30 p.m.: Bedtime

BREAKFAST OF
CHAMPIONS

No trip to Kye Gompa would be complete without the breakfast combination of Butter Tea (also known as 'gur gur chai' due to the sound it makes when churned) and Puk. There also might not be a more divisive dish than Butter Tea if your idea of tea conflicts with one that is buttery and salty. Very buttery and salty. So let's take tea as a misnomer and call this bad boy a soup instead?

A core team of three individuals, often accompanied by little ones, are responsible for feeding 350 monks breakfast, lunch and dinner.

When the water is roiling over a fire, 'salty' tea leaves are added into the gargantuan pot. These tea leaves, resembling shredded bark, are often used specifically during Tibetan Buddhist ceremonies and are otherwise elusive in Spiti. But this practice is seen across northern India, Tibet and China where monks and villagers claim that these leaves have special properties. After the tea leaves have leeched their flavour into the water, the monks will remove them and top up the pot with fresh milk that comes from the dairy co-op below the monastery.

And now, the fun part: rhythmically churning butter into the tea. Lots of pure, fresh, butter.

At 8 a.m. sharp, the head chef-monk will step into the courtyard and sound the breakfast alarm: a conch shell. And at last it is time to taste your creation: a strangely soothing, creamy, saltiness that slides down your throat, warming your body and lingering in the back of your mouth.

As you reach the last fourth of the 'tea', monks invite you to make Puk by adding sattu to the butter tea along with a touch of ghee and sugar, and kneading it into a dough-like substance.

This breakfast is not only surrounded by religious influences—first offering the chai to the hungry ghosts that wonder the monastery—but this meal is exactly what is required for the monks to survive the winter months: a warm and fatty 'soup' which quickly awakens your body and mind, along with the super-dense sattu that immediately satiates your hunger.

We can't speak to the special properties, but one of us felt the energy that morning . . . the other one took a nap.

THE BARE NECESSITIES

We once more boarded our handy Tempo Traveller as we followed the monks to a festival in the nearby Chichum village. Considered the town next door, the twists, turns, ups, bumps and towering bridges where you can't see the bottom puts Spiti's isolated nature into perspective.

Although Spiti did maintain contact with its neighbours, trading Spitian grain for Ladakhi salt,[42] this isolation had many consequences for the cuisine. The food systems in Spiti are largely self-sustaining, where each household either has direct access to the three pillars—dairy, grain and meat—or knows someone they can mooch off of.

As we reached Chichum, finally hoping for the first glance of all the monks in one place with celebrations abounding, we learnt that it was to actually start the next day, and instead detoured to Kibber to meet the farmer Dorje, who goes by the name Chengez Khan. (Which is a touchy topic since our biggest regret on this trip would probably have to be not being able to ask how Dorje came to be called Chengez.)

DAIRY

A Jersey cow was bred with a yak, resulting in the Churu. The Churu breed, which now dominates the dairy scene, is blessed with the yak's creamier milk at the Jersey cow's quantity.

The dairy cycle begins with this churu milk. But other than to supplement teas, milk itself isn't heavily consumed. Instead, the addition of bacterial cultures and heat turns milk into yoghurt (dahi). The churning of yoghurt yields two products: lassi from the liquids and then butter or ghee from the solids. The lassi is then boiled to yield pala, a fresh cheese used in stuffings, toppings or chutneys.

As we toured Chengez's house, he took us to his roof where most of the pala was being dried into churpe for safe-keeping during their winter hibernation. Most thukpas here have churpe as one of the bases. You'll find churpe stuffed into momos. Finely ground churpe will even be used as a grain substitute.[43]

And some will snack on it like a cheesy chewing gum.

GRAINS

From the days of trade with Ladakh, barley has been ubiquitous in Spiti—gifts, religious offerings and everyday meals. *Anaaj*, or grains, are the largest form of donations that come into the monastery.

Beginning with April, the crop rotations in the valley form 2-3 month cycles ending in late September. The following harvest is called *mandai* in which the entire village comes together to rampage over the crops with tractors—separating the barley pearls from the grass.

BARLEY'S AVATARS

There's **whole barley**, which is exactly what you think it is. Then **broken barley** which is used in soups or porridge. **Tsampa** is barley that's been roasted then ground into flour (also known as sattu). And lastly, **Jenpe** is a finely ground flour that's used as an addition to thukpas. Then come the preparations:

Puk: a simple mixture of warm water, salt and sattu. The sattu powder is added to a liquid and hand kneaded into a dry, doughy substance. Commonly seen in the monastery kitchens where sattu is mixed into the butter tea.

Zara: a more refined version of Puk where one-part water to two parts grain will be added to a pot to boil together with salt. The results will be similar to halwa and is served in round lumps formed by pressing the zara into a large serving spoon.

Pheymar: think a sweet version of Puk or Zara. You can use either form of preparation, just with the addition of ghee and sugar instead of salt. The resulting mixture is then rolled into rounds, like laddoos.

Daliya: a simple porridge from broken barley boiled in water or milk—either sweet or salty—and consumed for breakfast.

CHAANG

Chaang, the moonshine of Spiti, would be our choice for the fourth of these dietary pillars. It is also associated with faith, for when Chengez Khan served us he would first slide a glob of ghee on the rim as an offering to *preta*, the hungry ghost.

Chaang is produced from barley and rice through the addition of Phab, a traditional yeast in Himachal Pradesh. If you are looking for something more hardcore, you could try Arrak—a clear high proof alcohol that's made by distilling Chaang. It packs quite the punch.[44,45] On our last night, drinking with Chengez, one shot of Arrak was enough to warm our bodies and send us into a heated conversation about something we don't remember any more. With Chaang, as with Spitian living, there is no creation of waste. The leftover fermented grains are dried and ground to create either a sour flour or food for livestock. Unfortunately, there's not much alcohol left in the grains at this point, so don't bank on running into any tipsy cows.

MEAT

It's normal to think that meat consumption wouldn't be a norm of a Buddhist community, but this is one of the local flavours Buddhism has developed in Spiti. Fewer resources combined with a cold desert climate, as Chengez explains, means they had to look for nutrition wherever they could—especially a protein that could be preserved for winter.

The monks tell us that until roughly two years ago, meat used to be cooked and consumed in Kye. A push towards healthier eating habits has reduced consumption, but they are still free to eat meat outside the grounds. Sheep is consumed year round, either fresh or dried, while the meat from the larger animals, such as Churu or yak, is reserved for winter. Chicken has been introduced but is

only found in some of the larger towns such as Kaza due to tourism.

The importance of these animals isn't limited to food. Rather, the additional products that stem from livestock have long connected them to Spitian life: simple resources like rope, tools, or clothing from the wool.

TO PEA,
OR NOT TO PEA

Today, Spiti is undergoing a major change: shifting away from traditional crops, such as black peas, towards cash crops, like green peas. Even Kye Gompa has turned green, these peas forming an increasing fraction of their produce sold to support the monastery.

Black peas (not to be confused with the Grammy winning Black Eyed Peas known for *My Humps*), are indigenous to Spitian lands. Its low water requirement and hardiness make it a perfect fit for Spiti's rugged soil.

With its higher water and labour requirements, green peas have a lower profit margin when compared to a crop like barley. Moreover, the green pea wasn't built for these lands, and thus, it's susceptibility to the climate and critters has brought pesticides and fertilizers into the valley—diminishing the once organic and eco-friendly farms.

For India, where diabetes is now rampant, the inclusion of holistic ingredients is becoming a necessity. If the demand for barley or black peas, crops already integral to Spiti increased, then farmers could go back to producing them, a simple shift that is good for their wallets, good for Indian agriculture and especially good for all of our bellies.

They needed marketing, so here it is.

MUTTON
MOMOS
(Serves 4)

We finally reached Chichum village. While
Devang started to click pictures, I got cozy
with the momo-making aunties. I had finally
infiltrated the inner circle of this village, where
after singing a song with my name randomly
thrown in, we moved on to gossip.

Today's topic: Devang's "feminine" dhoti
pants.

Ingredients
Dough
1 cup refined flour | ¼ tsp salt | ½ tsp oil
¼ cup water

Filling
1 whole red onion, minced
1 tbsp gemune (or dried garlic or onion leaves)
2 cups ground mutton
¼ cup pala (or paneer)
1 tsp ghee | Salt (to taste)

Mix the flour, salt and oil in a large bowl. Slowly add water as needed, kneading vigorously, until you have a soft dough.

Set the dough aside for 20–30 minutes, covered, in a cool, dark Batcave-like place.

Heat a pan over medium flame and sauté the onions and gemune with a touch of ghee until they begin to brown. Add salt to taste.

Add the ground mutton and cook, stirring occasionally, until the meat is no longer pink, but still juicy.

Turn off the heat, mix in the pala or paneer.

Take your dough and roll it into long cylindrical segments. Break off pieces roughly the size of Ferrero Rocher chocolates (small 3–4 cm balls.)

Take a ball and flatten it in the palm of your hand. Then, starting in the middle, gently begin to press down while rotating the dough, thinning the dough as you work your way outside. The outer edges should be fairly thin while maintaining a little thickness towards the middle.

Spoon some of the stuffing inside, enough to only fill the centre thicker part of the shell. Fold the dough into a pattern of your choosing. Start by folding over the dough and pinching the two ends together on one corner, gently working your way around.

Steam for around 15 minutes or until the momos no longer stick to the bottom of the pan.

Serve hot with chutney.

THUKPA

Thukpa means soup. It's very important that you understand that going forward. Thukpa equals soup. Just as pasta can refer to a plethora of different dishes and preparations, Thukpa is no different. This warm, comforting and carby meal is usually eaten either for breakfast or dinner.

The Many-Faced Thukpa

Semthuk
The simplest preparation in which sattu is mixed into the soup base right before taking it off the heat.

Chindook
broken barley is added to the soup base and boiled alongside the fellow vegetables.

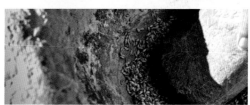

Thenthuk
the version of thukpa you are most likely to see in restaurants, with long refined flour rectangular noodles. This dough follows the same recipe above for momos with superfine atta.

Shunali
use the momo recipe, but replace the salt and oil with ghee and sugar. Form a dough in the shape of a longer cylinder roughly 1 cm thick. Break off long cylindrical pieces and boil them in your soup base.

Baksal
use the momo recipe, but substitute sattu. Form the dough in the shape of a long cylinder, roughly 2 cm thick. Break off short round pieces and boil them in your soup base. (If you prepare the dough with atta, you get what is called **Keu**.)

Thukpa Tadka

A tadka is roasted spices or flavourings in oil that is mixed into the thukpa at the very end to add heat, herbiness and a bit of that room-filling burnt-smell goodness. This will make or break your thukpa.

For the oil, choose ghee, rendered animal fat, sesame oil or mustard oil. For the flavourings, the absolute best tadka we had was made with gemune, or a pungent oniony herb, but chances are this herb will be hard to procure so opt for garlic or onion leaves. And for the spice, choose from what's typically found in the Indian pantry such as fenugreek, cumin or coriander.

Semthuk of Chichum village
(Serves 4)

Only a couple hours after we chowed down on momos, the village once more returned to the empty building that had been converted into a makeshift kitchen for the day to begin the preparation of this thukpa—now cooking with torches and headlights.

INGREDIENTS
8 cups water
1 cup churpe (or dried paneer)
½ cup dried spinach
½ cup sliced radish
½ cup pala (or paneer)
1 cup sattu (roasted barley flour)
Salt to taste

Set the water to boil in a large pot.
Once the water begins to roil, add the churpe and let it boil for 20 minutes.
Add the dried spinach and chopped radish and let it cook through, about 10 minutes.
Add the pala, sattu and salt and simmer for another 5 minutes. Serve hot.

Baksal of Chengez Khan
(Serves 4)

On the other hand, this thukpa has a bit more zing to it, as the saying we just made up goes: like thukpa, like person.

INGREDIENTS
Soup Base
8 cups water | 1 cup churpe (or dried paneer)
1 tsp rendered sheep fat
½ cup gemune (dried garlic or onion leaves)

Baksal
½ cup refined flour
½ cup sattu (roasted barley flour)
¼ cup gemune (onion or garlic leaves)
¼ tsp salt | ½ tsp oil | ¼ cup water

Set the water to boil in a large pot.
Once the water begins to roil, add the churpe and let it boil for 20 minutes.
Prepare your baksal in the meantime by combining all the ingredients together and kneading them into a dough.
Roll out the dough into long strands roughly 2 cm in diameter.
Tear off pieces at roughly 2 cm intervals and add them into the thukpa. Add salt to taste and cook for 20 minutes.
Prepare the tadka by roasting gemune into rendered sheep fat on low heat for 2 minutes, until the gemune has just started to burn.
Pour a bit of the soup base into the pan with the tadka, before adding the entire tadka back into your soup.

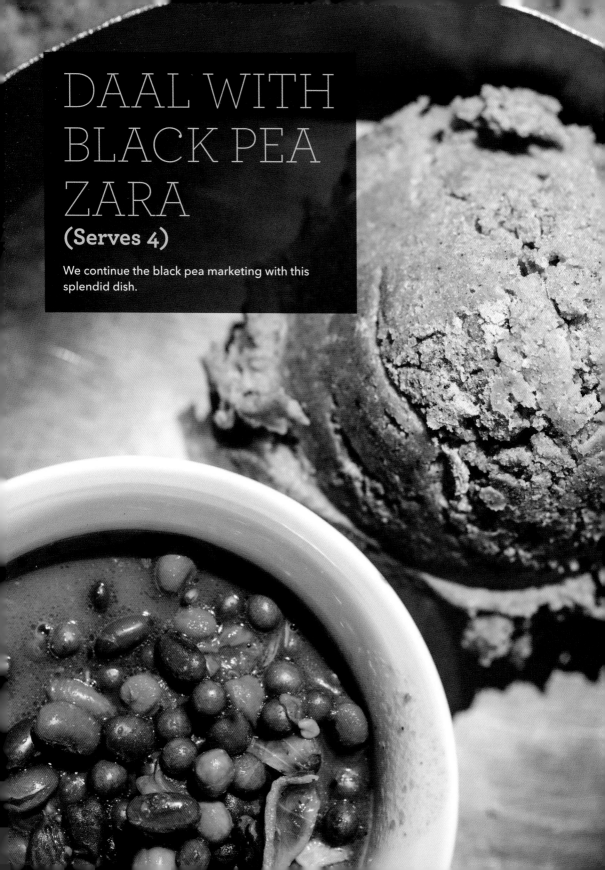

DAAL WITH BLACK PEA ZARA

(Serves 4)

We continue the black pea marketing with this splendid dish.

Mixed Daal

Ingredients
½ cup black peas
½ cup red kidney beans
1 tsp salt
1 tbsp oil
1 red onion, chopped
3 cloves garlic, chopped
1 green chilli, sliced
1 tsp cumin
1 tsp turmeric
1 tsp coriander seeds
1 tsp carom seeds
1 tomato, chopped

Soak the lentils overnight. Drain the water.
Add salt and then pressure-cook the peas and
beans for 20 minutes with roughly 2 cups of
water.
Prepare the tadka by warming the oil over low
heat. Add the onions, garlic, chilli and spices.
As soon as the tadka begins to sputter, add the
tomatoes to the pan and some more salt (to
taste).
Add the pressure-cooked lentils. Let it cook until
the gravy is as thick or thin as you please.

Zara

Ingredients
2 cups water
1 cup ground black peas (or another pulse
flour)
3 cups sattu
1 tsp salt

Set the water to boil in a pan.
Add the ground black peas and sattu, along
with salt.
Keep stirring as the grains absorb the water and
the mixture thickens and attains a halwa-like
consistency.

EPILOGUE

A haze had fallen over the city when the three weary travellers returned. As with most *once upon a time* tales, these musketeers had embarked on a mystical task: travelling in search of the Food of the Gods. From the foothills of Meghalaya to the coast of Udvada, the feasts of Jagannath to the comforts of Spiti—the muse of Penguin would carry their stories for the years to come.

But now they were back in the place known as New Delhi, and the haze that surrounded them—pollution. Varud son of Ghee Wala searched for an Uber. Devang of the Singh Clan sorted through missed calls. Toni, Sir Man Friday, rolled a joint.

Through this saga, they had very much championed objectivity, tried to avoid distorting cultures, peoples and pasts through their own lens. All through, they were very much unaware of the journey—learning, exploring, or suffering the wrath of the Yummy Belly Syndrome.

But they didn't consider how they would have the largest impact in telling the story itself. And in turn, become a part of a narrative in which each page could hold a chapter of its own.

This was a power they didn't want; they had merely stumbled on to it. To influence stories as old as time is a burdening task for mortals. But now that they had, as Uncle Ben had said, *With great power comes great responsibility*.

As they loaded the car, everything returned to the way it once was. But none could voice what was unanimously felt. A feeling, a void. Completing a journey, as with a book, is unsettling. The sensation, lingering in your belly, finally comes to words. A simple question:

Now what?

The thing with stories is that they never end.
And often, the last line is the most underwhelming.

THANK YOU

Like any good parent knows, it takes a village to bring a love-child as this book into the world. (In the case of Rongmesek, literally.)

In Spiti, Kishore Thukral helped us navigate the lands when this book was a lowly sample chapter. His Eminence T.K. Lochen Tulku Rinpoche and Sonam Angdui (Nono) helped us connect with the community. Dorje Tsering (Chengez Khan) and Tsering Dorje (Chhotu) brought us into their homes. In Udvada, Marzban Hathiram remained patient with us as we battled with ignorance. The Globe Hotel family who shared their food with outsiders.

In Odisha, Vicky Rastogi whose passion behind faith got us to Jagannath. And Haribol Singhari, Padma Mahavir and Dr Abhay Kumar Nayak who helped us explore the different dimensions once there.

In Kolkata, Ms A.M. Cohen whose sassy sense of humour brought warmth into the hollowed synagogues. Jael and Flower Silliman, without whose work we'd have nothing to say. And Saldana's Bakery for their delicious time.

In Rongmesek, the Lyngdoh brothers (Dr Fabian and Constantine) for their sincerity and jubilance. Albinus Timung and Morningkeey Phangcho for their energy and commitment to the community. And Michael Shadap and Esther M. Sawian for helping us find them.

To those in and around the studio: Yash Pal Singh, Prerna Shekhar, Shreya Sarawagi, Yash Pal Singh, Japneesh Kholi, Anjali Hans, Prateeq Kumar, Vidur Gupta, Ayushi Rastogi, Mohd Kalam, Amit Sharma and Vimal Rawat. Oh and Yash Pal Singh (aka Toni).

A special thanks to Keshav Suri and The Lalit Hotel Group for their continued support in this endeavour.

Gurveen, our editor. You rock. Like seriously though.

And the friends and family who have inspired, supported and most importantly taught us—even at the risk of their sanity.

To everyone, a sincerest of sincere thank yous.

Sources

RONGMESEK, MEGHALAYA / KARBI TRIBE

1. Teron, Dharamsing. 'Understanding the Karbi Folk Religion'. Karbis of Assam, 2008. https://karbi.wordpress.com/2008/02/26/understanding-the-karbi-folkreligion/#more-56.
2. Fr Otto Hopfenmuller. Sds.Org, 2018. http://www.sds.org/about-us/greatsalvatorians/otto-hopfenmueller/.
3. Shodhganga.Inflibnet.Ac.In, 2012. http://shodhganga.inflibnet.ac.in/bitstream/10603/67733/7/07_chapter%202.pdf.
4. Shodhganga.Inflibnet.Ac.In, 2012. http://shodhganga.inflibnet.ac.in/bitstream/10603/67733/7/07_chapter%203.pdf
5. Teron, Dharamsing. 'Teron, a Karbi Kitchen—From Tradition to Modernity'. Karbis ofAssam, 2009. https://karbi.wordpress.com/2009/10/17/inside-a-karbi-kitchen-fromtradition-to-modernity/#more-161.

UDVADA, GUJARAT / IRANSHAH ATASH BEHRAM

6. http://www.iranicaonline.org/articles/iransah
7. Manekshaw, B.J. Parsi Food and Customs. New Delhi: Penguin Books India, 1996.
8. Wall text for Zorastrian Faith and Culture. Udvada, Gujarat: Zoroastrian Museum & Information Centre.
9. Manekshaw. Parsi Food and Customs.
10. 'The Secret Ingredient to My Personality| Anahita Dhondy | TEDxShivNadarUniversity'. YouTube video. Posted by 'Tedx Talks'. 17:15. 2017. https://www.youtube.com/watch?v=-tH75fkJorc.
11. Wall text for Zorastrian Faith and Culture. Udvada, Gujarat: Zoroastrian Museum & Information Centre.
12. Pollan, Michael. Cooked. New York: Penguin, 2013.

KOLKATA, WEST BENGAL / MAGHEN DAVID SYNAGOGUE

13. Palmach, Treasure. 'Creative Commons Immigration to Israel'. The Palmach images Photo Gallery is licensed under CC BY 2.0/ Desaturated from original;
14. 'The Last Jews of Kolkata | Unique Stories from India'. YouTube video. Posted by '101 India'. 7:33. 2016. https://www.youtube.com/watch?v=TRqXVbu52Ao;
15. Silliman, Jael. 'To Kolkata, From Baghdadi Jews, With Love'. The Wire, 22 July 2017. https://thewire.in/food/from-baghdad-with-love.
16. Solomon, Sally. '03 Notable Members of and from the Community—Shalom Aaron Cohen'. From Hooghly Tales. London: David Ashley Publishing, 1998. pp. 57–58. Jewishcalcutta.in.
http://www.jewishcalcutta.in/exhibits/show/notable_members/sh_aaron_cohen
17. NATMO. 'Map Of Jewish Calcuttata'. Jewishcalcutta.in, 1998.
http://www.jewishcalcutta.in/exhibits/show/21-map-of-jewish-calcutta.
18. Marks, Zach. 'The Last Jews Of Kolkata'. India Ink. The New York Times, 2013. https://india.blogs.nytimes.com/2013/10/24/the-last-jews-of-kolkata.

19. Wasko, Dennis. 'The Jewish Palate: The Baghdadi Jews of Calcutta, India'. The Jerusalem Post, 2011. https://www.jpost.com/Food-Index/The-Jewish-Palate-The-Baghdadi-Jews-of-Calcutta-India.

20. Tandon, Rahul. 'The Last Jews of Calcutta'. BBC News, 28 March 2014. http://www.bbc.co.uk/religion/0/26740099

21. Schechter, Solomon, Julius H. Greenstone, Emil G. Hirsch and Kaufmann Kohler. 'Dietary Laws'. JewishEncyclopedia.com. http://www.jewishencyclopedia.com/articles/5191-dietary-laws.

22. 'Definition of tamarind In English'. Oxforddictionaries.com. https://en.oxforddictionaries.com/definition/tamarind.

23. Silliman, Flower. Three Cups of Flower. Kolkata: Sadhana Press, 2014;

24. Silliman. 'To Kolkata, From Baghdadi Jews, With Love';

25. Silliman, Flower. '15 Calcutta Jewish Cuisine: A Taste of Jewish Cuisine'. Jewishcalcutta.in, 2018. http://www.jewishcalcutta.in/exhibits/show/food/a-noteon-jewish-cooking--flow.

26. Leiman, Sid Z. 'Jewish Religious Year'. Encyclopedia Britannica, 2018. https://www.britannica.com/topic/Jewish-religious-year.

27. Ibid.

28. Silliman. Three Cups of Flower.

PURI, ODISHA / SHREE JAGANNATH TEMPLE

29. Pradhan, R.C. Sri Jagannath: Enigmatic Lord The Universe. Bhubaneshwar: Sisukalam;

30. "Konark | India'. Encyclopedia Britannica, 2018. https://www.britannica.com/place/Konark.

31. 'Odisha | History, Map, Population & Facts'. Encyclopedia Britannica, 2018, https://www.britannica.com/place/Odisha.

32. 'Ashoka | Emperor Of India'. Encyclopedia Britannica, 2018, https://www.britannica.com/biography/Ashoka.

33. 'Odisha | History, Map, Population & Facts'. Encyclopedia Britannica, 2018, https://www.britannica.com/place/Odisha.

34. Devi, Bandita. 'Some Aspects Of British Administration In Orissa'. Delhi: Academic Foundation, 1992.

35. Kumar Nayak, Jatindra. 'Hubback's Memoirs'. Telegraph, 29 November 2010, https://www.telegraphindia.com/1101129/jsp/orissa/story_13234116.jsp.

36. 'Odisha | History, Map, Population & Facts'. Encyclopedia Britannica, 2018, https://www.britannica.com/place/Odisha.

37. Butler, Stephanie. 'Off The Spice Rack: The Story Of Pepper'. History, 17 January 2013, https://www.history.com/news/off-the-spice-rack-the-story-of-pepper.

38. Pradhan, Sri Jagannath: Enigmatic Lord The Universe.

SPITI, HIMACHAL PRADESH / KYE GOMPA

39. 'Key Monastery Road Sign'. Gelukpa School. Spiti.

40. Singh, Vijay Kumar. Sects In Tibetan Buddhism. New Delhi: D.K. Printworld, 2006.

41. Ibid.

42. Rizvi, Janet. Peasant-Traders of Ladakh: A Study In Oral History. 12th ed.
    New Delhi: India International Centre, 1985.

43. Bhalla, Tek Chand and Savitri. 'Traditional Foods and Beverages of Himachal
    Pradesh.'Shimla: Himachal Pradesh University, 2007,
    http://nopr.niscair.res.in/bitstream/123456789/815/1/IJTK%206%281%29%20
    %282007%29%2017-24.pdf.

44. Kanwar, S.S., M.K. Gupta, Chhaya Katoch, Rajeev Kumar and Promila Kanwar.
    'Traditional Fermented Foods of Lahaul and Spiti Area of Himachal Pradesh'.
    Palampur: Departments of Microbiology and Home Science Extension Education,
    CSK Himachal Pradesh Krishi Vishvavidyalaya, 2007.
    http://www.niscair.res.in/sciencecommunication/ResearchJournals/rejour/ijtk/
    Fulltextsearch/2007/January%202007/IJTK-Vol%206(1)-January%202007-pp%20
    42-45.htm.

45. Bhalla and Savitri. 'Traditional Foods and Beverages of Himachal Pradesh'.